HAWAII'S Humpbacks
Unveiling the Mysteries

HUMPBACKS

MAMMALS Like us

SUMMER FEEDERS

Migrations

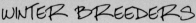

WINTER BREEDERS

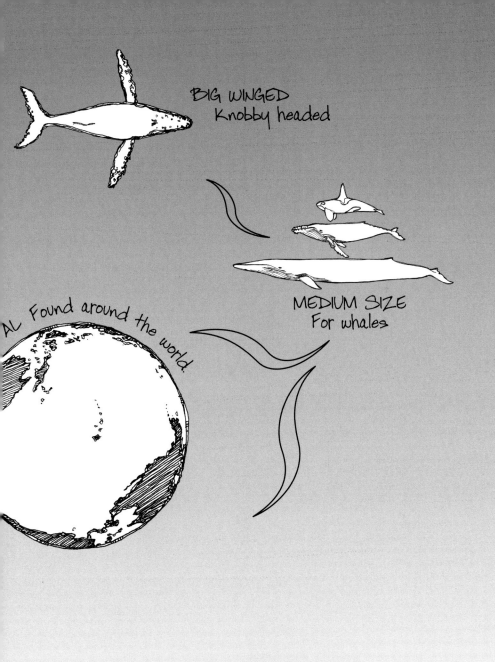

BIG WINGED
Knobby headed

MEDIUM SIZE
For whales

AL Found around the world

RECOVERING
From whaling.

HAWAII'S Humpbacks
Unveiling the Mysteries

Jim Darling

PHOTOGRAPHS BY Flip Nicklin

ILLUSTRATIONS BY Susan W. Barnes

Granville Island Publishing

Library and Archives Canada Cataloguing in Publication

Darling, James David, 1950–
    Hawaii's humpbacks : unveiling the mysteries : the ultimate guide for whale watching / Jim Darling.

Includes bibliographical references and index.
ISBN 978-1-894694-59-9

    1. Humpback whale. 2. Humpback whale--Hawaii. I. Title.

QL737.C424D37 2009   599.5'25   C2009-900151-9

Editors: Graham Hayman and Christine Laurin
Indexer: Bookmarks
Photos: Flip Nicklin (except where otherwise credited)
Illustrator: Susan Wallace Barnes
Graphics: Josie Cleland
Photo preparation and design concepts: Gary Wilcox
Cover designer: Joan Selix Berman

Granville Island Publishing Ltd.
212-1656 Duranleau St · Granville Island
Vancouver BC · Canada · V6H 3S4
info@granvilleislandpublishing.com
www.granvilleislandpublishing.com

First published March 2009
Printed in China

*   *   *

Photographs taken under the authority of National Marine Fisheries Service (NMFS) scientific research permits:

    Permit 987 & 753-1599 (Flip Nicklin, Jim Darling, Meagan Jones, Bill Scott)
    Permit 313-1772 01 (Mark Ferrari)
    Permit 932-1489 (Ed Lyman)

Contents

Acknowledgements

I gratefully acknowledge the key role played by Bob and Pat Steinhoff, who offered inspiration and support for this project during a cruise in Alaska. Their commitment during its development is much appreciated. Sadly, Pat has since passed away and this book memorializes her love of the ocean and the creatures in it.

Whale Trust provided critical, continuing support for this book, which has taken several years to complete. Special thanks to Meagan Jones, who administered the project and also reviewed it and contributed to its content, Bill Scott, who kept things organized financially, and Allen Jones, who advised on marketing.

Whale Trust is extremely grateful to Makana Aloha Foundation for providing a significant portion of the funds for this book.

Flip Nicklin's photographs and Susan Wallace Barnes's illustrations enhance this book tremendously. The donation of their work is typical of their generous support for whale research and education. Many of Flip's photographs were provided through his agency, Minden Pictures, and special thanks are due to Larry Minden and Chris Carey. *National Geographic* magazine graciously allowed the use of several photographs from past articles on humpback whales.

This book is partially based on a technical report, *Characterization of Humpback Whale Behavior in Hawaii*, completed for the Hawaiian Islands Humpback Whale National Marine Sanctuary (HIHWNMS) in 1999 by the author. Thanks are due to Jeff Walters (HIHWNMS co-coordinator) for his role in the initial report.

Additional photographs were contributed by Meagan Jones and Bill Scott (both from Whale Trust), Mark Ferrari (Center For Whale Studies), Ed Lyman (HIHWNMS and NOAA Fisheries Marine Mammal Health and Stranding Program), John Ford on behalf of the late Gordon Pike (Fisheries and Oceans Canada), Koji Nakamura (Japan Underwater Films), Jason A. Moore, Ed Lane, Greg Silber and Fran Gealer. Thank you.

General support for the author (allowing me time to write) came from Sarah Crandall Haney (Canadian Whale Institute) and Gregory Colbert (Flying Elephants Foundation), and is enormously appreciated.

I would also like to take this opportunity to thank the Maui residents who have helped us on many different fronts, for years (decades, actually), including Ron and Diane Roos, Jim Luckey, Tad and Cindy Luckey, Mark and Jeri Robinson, Barry and Irene McPhee, Connie Sutherland and the late Chuck Sutherland. In addition, I thank the many volunteers who have assisted us in the field over the years (please see www.whaletrust.org for names). Most particularly, special thanks are due Karen Miller and Jason Sturgis.

As always, the key to this and all Whale Trust projects is the donors. Their support is greatly appreciated. Space constraints prevent us from naming everyone (please see website), however, a special acknowledgement is due Darlene and Jeff Anderson, Flip Nicklin, Garry Weber, Allen and Ann Jones, Pat and Karyn Cochran, Margaret Sears, Bill Scott, and Mary Whitney and Betsy Collins (Fluke Foundation).

I wish to acknowledge the Granville Island Publishing team in Vancouver (BC), including Jo Blackmore, Graham Hayman, Christine Laurin, Gary Wilcox, François Trahan, Elspeth Richmond, Neall Calvert and Rachel Moffat. Josie Cleland of Lightwave Image Services in Nanaimo (BC) produced the book's graphics and Joan Selix Berman in Maui designed the cover.

As with any project like this, the innocent victims of the author's preoccupation are family and friends. I thank them for their patience and support.

Finally, this book could not have been written without the collective work of dedicated researchers in Hawaii over the last thirty years. I acknowledge their endeavors and hope I have done them justice.

Foreword

For over thirty years now, researchers from around the world have come to study whales in Hawaii. This book is about what we have learned . . . and not learned. It is meant for both novice and experienced whale watchers. For the former, it provides humpback whale basics, answers some questions (or perhaps explains why we can't answer them yet), and hopefully encourages your interest. For the experienced whale watcher (and there are many), this book lets you in on what researchers are doing and thinking. It presents some of the puzzles, challenges, and current hypotheses about whale behavior seen every day through the winter. In either case, whether you're a beginner or a veteran, the intention is for this book to deepen your knowledge about these remarkable creatures with which we share Hawaiian waters.

Humpback whale studies conducted in Hawaii are the basis of this book, with information extracted from over fifty references from the 1970s to the present. In addition, information from selected studies from other regions (many of which have addressed similar or related research questions and add to the discussion of humpback behavior) has been included. Where all the studies relevant to a topic agree, summary statements are made. Where differences in interpretations and alternative ideas have arisen, the arguments for them are introduced and questions that remain open noted. All of the references that provide further information or discussion on the topic are included in the Sources section at the end of the volume.

The information in this book comes from published scientific journals, graduate (MS and PhD) dissertations, technical reports, and several personal communications from researchers. It does not include unpublished field notes or manuscripts in the publication pipeline, all likely to provide exciting new information. Our intention is to reprint this book periodically with the latest updates.

This book is a little different from most. The goal has been to stay very true to what the studies have told us, but also to include some of the research process — the multiple ideas or hypotheses (some eventually proven, many ultimately discarded), as well as the compelling questions that push research forward.

For the non-scientist, it can be frustrating at times when you expect short, simple, black-and-white answers to what seem like basic questions about whales (e.g. Why do they sing? or Why do they breach?). Most researchers have had the experience of a TV documentary director trying desperately to get a concise reply to a question that does not yet have one, although often an 'answer' gets provided to the audience in the editing room! This book doesn't do that, and the hope is you will find it more interesting because of it.

Jim Darling

Chapter 1

Whales!

WHALES! If you have been to Maui (or to any of the Hawaiian Islands) in winter, odds are you have seen humpback whales. In fact, between Christmas and Easter, it's hard to look out to sea and *not* see whales. This is their winter home. Sometimes it takes a few minutes of searching to spot quiet, lone or paired adults offering only puffy blows and a brief glimpse of a back or tail. Other times, splashes from slapping flukes or flippers, the explosions of breaches, or groups of a dozen or so whales racing around in tight formation will grab anyone's attention from miles away.

Everyone sees them, from commuters making the daily trek along the coast, to kids playing on the beach, vacationers lounging on their lanai, waiters moving from bar to table, or local business folks sipping iced tea in one of the waterfront restaurants. They stop what they are doing for a moment (or an hour) to watch, and then continue on with their day. Even if you don't glance out to sea once in a while and are completely unaware of the whales, chances are you will still get caught in Hawaii's unique whale jams, with hundreds of cars pulling to the side of the road (often wildly) to gaze at nearshore action. Hawaii's whales are world-class spectacular and more — they are part of the background, the ambience of the islands.

What Are They Doing Out There?

Humpbacks in Hawaii, both male and female, are trying to pass their genes on to the next generation, if necessary depriving their neighbors of the same opportunity! Virtually all of the behavior we see and hear is part of this ultimate objective. It's critical, complex, and fascinating.

From our knowledge to date, humpback whales appear to be typical mammals in this regard. Individual males go for quantity — that is, to sire as many offspring as possible (preferably all of them). Females, on the other hand, are presumably more interested in quality — finding

During winter it is hard to miss the whales cavorting off Hawaii's shorelines — there are thousands of them.

the most fit male to be the father. There is conflict and resolution within, and between, the sexes.

Hawaii's waters, therefore, swirl with complex social behavior. The whales follow strategies, interact, and form relationships. Individual whales may search, attract, avoid, compete, and cooperate, always weighing off energy cost versus reproductive gain. This drama is on display whenever the whales are in Hawaii, for in the midst of all this they jump and roll and splash and race . . .

The 1970s

Biologists knew very little about 'Hawaiian' humpback whales at the beginning of the 1970s. At the outset, we did not know where these whales came from, where they went, how many were out there, when they were present, and not a single word had been written describing behavior patterns that are popular lore today. In fact, prior to the 1970s, there was little general awareness (public or scientific) that the whales were even in Hawaii!

Whaling of humpback whales had ceased in the northeast Pacific a few years earlier, in 1966. It's not known why, but humpbacks were not actually hunted in Hawaii. In fact, Hawaii may well be the only whale grounds in the North Pacific where there is no history of commercial whaling. (This is so unusual that some researchers wonder if humpbacks even came to Hawaii during whaling times — the peak humpback whaling era covering the first half of the 1900s. Frankly, this is the most likely explanation for the lack of whaling history.)

Throughout the rest of the North Pacific, however, humpback whale populations, which may have included 'Hawaiian' whales, were subjected to relentless hunting for over fifty years. Indeed, commercial extinction (when commercial whaling operations were no longer viable due to difficulty in finding a whale) occurred in most

Whale watching off Maui began in the 1970s. It was an opportunity for people to see living whales and for the whales to interact with humans not bent on killing them.

I Was the Intruder . . .

"There was not a breath of wind and the sea was glassy calm. . . . I eased off the surfboard. . . . One instant the water was empty. The next, it had substance. A vague, looming shadow became the outline of a tremendous head. . . . All feelings of apprehension vanished. The monster from the depths had appeared, but . . . he was not frightening. In fact he seemed to radiate friendliness. . . . The whale did not change his pace or seem disturbed. But he did roll to one side for a better view of me. . . . I was the intruder, a curiosity from another world."

— Jon Lindbergh
Life magazine, 1967

This may be the earliest published description of an underwater encounter with a 'Hawaiian' humpback (off Lahaina, Maui), several years ahead of general interest in these whales.

regions before international protection. We're not sure how many 'Hawaiian' humpbacks remained by then — a few hundred, maybe.

Then came the 1970s, and our view of whales changed — about as much as it could change. As the decade began, the first killer whales had been brought to aquariums and captured public attention. Then Jacques Cousteau's TV documentaries introduced us all to living whales in their natural habitat. The songs of humpback whales were played around the world on bestselling record albums (and were even sent into space). "Save the Whales" campaigns, with perhaps the first engagement of the mass media in conservation issues, brought the whales' plight to the forefront. The campaigns of Greenpeace and others received unprecedented coverage and interest. The art, and business, of whale watching truly began. The US Marine Mammal Protection Act was passed. The International Whaling Commission, long charged with the role of managing whaling, also became a forum for protecting whales. The more we got to know the animals as living creatures rather than as carcasses on a whaling ramp or as market commodities, the more our attitudes changed.

In that time and atmosphere, a few brave souls ventured out and slipped into the water with humpback whales. The first underwater photographs and films of whales in the blue, shimmering

Living humpback whales were first filmed in Hawaii in the 1970s, and those images did much to capture public attention. Above, a diver films a passing whale with a huge IMAX camera.

waters of Hawaii changed our perception of the world a little. These images, more than any other single factor, solidified human interest in the living whales.

The decade of the seventies also marked the beginning of an entirely new field of endeavor — the study of living whales in their natural habitat. Until that time, the idea that a researcher could locate and spend enough time with whales at sea to actually learn something about them was thought to be impossible. Research on live whales began with people who didn't know it could not be done. They sought out and spent time close to whales in their natural habitat. Soon it became clear that individual animals could be recognized by natural markings, allowing repeat sightings and extended observation. Within a decade of this discovery, such studies spanned the globe. Hawaii, along with a handful of other locations, was at the forefront of this activity.

The time since the 1970s has been one of unprecedented progress for whale research. With new tools and techniques (such as photo-identification, underwater observation, sophisticated genetic analysis of skin to determine sex and relationships, and high-tech satellite tracking), the horizons of what is possible have been extended over and over. It has been an exciting time for researchers, as virtually everything seen and documented has been new, providing the first real insights into the nature of living whales.

The Finest Natural Laboratory

Whales are found worldwide: along the coastlines of all the continents, around oceanic islands, amidst ice packs in polar seas, and far offshore. All these places are critical to whales. So, why study them in Hawaii? Because, hands down, it is one of the finest natural laboratories in the world.

There are significant challenges to studying wild whales. The top three are probably simply locating whales in the vast reaches of the sea, finding ocean conditions that allow a scientist to be more concerned with the project than survival, and then solving the logistics of spending the days, weeks, and months necessary to get the job done. It is critical that whales be studied in all locations, there is no doubt. However, the closer one is to overcoming these three challenges, the more time there is to explore the nature of the whales themselves.

Humpback whales typically seek out water in the 72–76°F (19–21°C) range for winter assembly. Such locations in the North Pacific are in the zone of the trade winds — so named for their consistency and strength, aiding the passage of sailing ships. In the northern hemisphere

Hawaii's warm, clear, and relatively calm waters make it one of the finest natural laboratories in the world.

'the trades' blow regularly from the northeast, typically at 15–35 knots. This is bad for whale researchers. Attempting to locate, stay close to, and study whales in these ocean conditions can be daunting, as can be attested by humpback researchers in many other locations in the world that have only low-lying or no land masses nearby.

In Hawaii, however, volcanic mountains ranging from 5,000 to 10,000 feet or more (1,500 to 3,000 m) (including the West Maui Mountains and Haleakala on Maui, and Mauna Loa and Mauna Kea on the Big Island) act as giant windbreaks and create calm-water zones (lees) behind them. Calm water is very good for whale research. (The size of the lee changes with wind speed and direction, and it is the first and most important subject of discussion every single morning of the field season.)

Another reason Hawaii is a prime location for whale research is its mid-ocean, subtropical location, which results in remarkable underwater visibility — not uncommonly in the 100-foot (30-m) range.

This visibility is the result of several factors, including a lack of large rivers to pour sediment in the water or supply nutrients for plankton growth — both of which reduce visibility. (However, run-off created from rainfall on agricultural lands does decrease visibility dramatically in the short term.) In Hawaii, the whales can actually be observed beneath the surface and, equally important, they can see us and not be surprised or frightened. Clearly, this is a huge advantage when studying whale behavior.

Last, but not least, are the very practical and logistical considerations that are a large part of any research program:

- How easy is it to reach the study area?
- Are there harbors with boat facilities, fuel, and services?
- What kind of accommodation is available?
- What language is spoken?
- Is it in a war zone?
- Are there medical facilities?
- How difficult is it going to be to actually get researchers on the water?
- What will the cost be?

These are significant limiting factors in many whale research programs around the world. In Hawaii, though, these issues are either relatively easily resolved or do not even arise.

It is the combination of all these things (lots of whales, calm conditions, good visibility, and logistical ease) that makes Hawaii so special in terms of whale research. Simply, it allows a researcher to spend entire days very close to whales, in conditions permitting observation both on the surface and underwater. These circumstances have led to a steady stream of research, photographs, and films, resulting in many first-descriptions, new insights, and new hypotheses on humpback behavior.

These conditions are also ideal for studies of other cetaceans. The list opposite illustrates the many other whales and dolphins that can be seen in Hawaii. Other species of large baleen whales are seen, but sightings are rare and usually fleeting. In contrast, a great variety of toothed whales (including dolphins) live here, with many species found where the banks surrounding the islands drop off into deep water.

Cetaceans in Hawaiian Waters

This list of cetaceans is a composite based on surveys of the Hawaiian Islands that have documented six species of baleen whales and eighteen species of toothed whales. The likelihood of sightings given here only suggests the odds of seeing a particular species during casual boating activities — it does not necessarily represent abundance of the species in Hawaii.

	Season(s) in Hawaii	Sightings
Baleen Whales (Mysticeti)		
Humpback Whale	Winter	Common
Right Whale	Winter	Rare
Minke Whale	Unknown	Rare
Bryde's Whale	Year-round	Rare
Sei Whale	Unknown	Rare
Fin Whale	Unknown	Rare
Toothed Whales (Odontoceti)		
Spotted Dolphin	Year-round	Common
Spinner Dolphin	Year-round	Common
Bottlenose Dolphin	Year-round	Common
False Killer Whale	Year-round	Common
Short-Finned Pilot Whale	Year-round	Common
Rough-Toothed Dolphin	Year-round	Common*
Melon-Headed Whale	Year-round	Common*
Pygmy Killer Whale	Year-round	Common*
Sperm Whale	Spring-Summer	Common*
Striped Dolphin	Year-round	Less Common
Pygmy Sperm Whale	Year-round	Less Common
Dwarf Sperm Whale	Unknown	Less Common
Blainville's Beaked Whale	Year-round	Rare
Cuvier's Beaked Whale	Year-round	Rare
Killer Whale	Unknown	Rare
Fraser's Dolphin	Unknown	Rare
Longman's Beaked Whale	Unknown	Rare
Risso's Dolphin	Unknown	Rare

In certain locations (e.g. Kona) sightings of this species are as stated; elsewhere, chances of seeing it are lower.

How Have We Learned About Humpback Whales?

Scientific understanding of humpback whales has come in two distinct phases: first, from the results of half a century of whaling, and second, from over thirty years of field studies of living whales.

Whaling Studies

For many years our knowledge of humpback whales came mostly from carcasses on whaling ramps.

Prior to research on living whales, virtually all we knew about their life history was pieced together from the examination of thousands of dead animals from whaling operations. Intrepid biologists, digging around inside dead whales, examined testes to learn the peak of male breeding activity (spermatogenesis), ovaries to determine female sexual maturity and birth rates, and fetus sizes to estimate birth times. Stomach contents told what they ate and when. The recovery of long metal darts (known as "Discovery tags") shot into whales in other locations determined where they had been prior to being killed.

Reports based on these data appeared from the early 1900s up to the 1960s and provided a valuable framework for understanding reproductive cycles; in fact, they are still used as a basis for studying the behavior of living whales.

Studying Living Whales at Sea

The second phase of whale study began in the 1970s with the first research on living whales in their natural habitat. The value of photo-identification of animals by natural markings to enable repeat sightings of individuals cannot be overstated. It remains the primary tool of living whale research. Close surface and underwater observations and the development of sighting and behavioral histories of individual whales gave rise to the first descriptions of behavior patterns in the wild.

Today, most whale research can be divided into three general approaches:

- *Short-term.* Includes surveys by boat or airplane that record location, numbers, general behavior (traveling, feeding, etc.), and perhaps social groupings. These studies are not based on individual IDs, are relatively short in duration, and provide snapshots of distribution and abundance over the survey area.

Whalers in Hawaii

Although no commercial whaling occurred in Hawaii, it was a popular place for whalers of the 1800s to spend the winter. The actual whaling, for sperm whales, occurred in northern seas in summer.

Lahaina, Maui was a favorite overwintering location, and clashes between whalers and missionaries make for colorful history.

Intriguingly, no mention of humpback whales has been found in the log books of whaling ships anchored in the roadstead off Lahaina. This makes some wonder if their presence in Hawaii in winter is a relatively new phenomenon.

Coincidentally, Lahaina is now the field base of the majority of whale research programs in Hawaii.

- *Long-term.* Includes abundance and distribution studies and all detailed behavior work. These studies are based on identification, repeat sightings, and extensive observations of individual whales. They are conducted over multiple years, even lifetimes, often from small craft and with both surface and under-water observations.

- *Remote.* Includes research on migration and behavior with satellite or other high-tech tags attached to the whales. These studies require relatively little time with the animal directly — just attaching the tag — but potentially huge amounts of time 'watching' remotely.

Due to its power in revealing the gender and relatedness of animals, the study of genetics is arguably a fourth approach in itself. However, it is more often an extra tool used in other studies. Researchers tend to specialize in one of these three approaches, or in genetics, as they all require somewhat different sets of expertise. Of course, ideally all these methods would be used to answer any specific question.

The approach taken to any whale study is determined by the objective — what exactly it is we are trying to learn. For example, common wildlife-management objectives are to estimate population size, map critical habitat, or determine age of sexual maturity and birth rate. In some cases, the objective is to define populations by studying migratory destinations and genetic relationships. In other cases, researchers may be primarily interested in the social organization and behavior of whales and address questions like:

- What is the mating system?
- What are the reproductive strategies of males and females?
- How (and what) do they communicate?
- What is the structure of whale society?

Researchers match the objective to the general approach, and set about designing the study.

Whales can be curious, too.
This whale takes a moment
to check out the researchers.

Many whale studies are conducted from small boats and involve photo-identifying animals and analyzing repeat sightings of individuals over many years. Above, one whale is releasing a stream of bubbles from its blowhole.

Working With Whales

Finding whales in a good study location is not the end to the challenges of studying whale behavior at sea — it's just the beginning. Think for a minute about the factors involved.

First, there is the ocean, which can change from calm to life threatening — at times in a matter of minutes. Then there are the whales themselves, with movements restricted by nothing except the shoreline and physiology, ranging over huge distances. Moreover, they spend 90 percent of their time hidden underwater.

Then there is the assortment of electrotechnical equipment such as digital cameras and recorders, hydrophones (underwater microphones), and GPS units that have become the mainstays of research and must work as they bounce around in damp, salty conditions on small boats. There are the boats themselves, prone to breakdowns and periodic downtime for maintenance.

The flow of a research season often goes something like this: Whales are present, but ocean is impossible; or ocean is calm but the whales are gone; or both whales and ocean are good but the boat breaks down; or everything is working but the rain last night ruined the visibility underwater. (You get the idea.) There are a number of variables, some entirely out of a researcher's control, which have to come together for the work to get done.

Consequently, studies of living whales at sea are long-term endeavors. It simply takes a long time to collect the observations necessary to be able to say anything with any level of scientific certainty. Usually, the more sophisticated the question (the goal is often to learn enough to ask more sophisticated questions), the more variables that need to line up before useful data is obtained, and therefore the more time is needed. Then, when everything works, we are rewarded with just a glimpse into the lives of these animals. To date, our understanding of whales comes from a series of such glimpses.

What Are Researchers Doing Out There?

From shore, or perhaps from a whale-watching boat, small boats may be seen operating very close to the whales. These are researchers. In Hawaii they are required to have federal and state permits to approach whales. The interaction of the researchers with whales (and consequent movements of the boats) depends on what they are trying to accomplish. Following are descriptions of several of the most common activities of researchers in Hawaii, including what may be seen from shore or a whale-watching boat, the technique(s) employed, and the use of the resulting data.

Who Studies Whales in Hawaii?

Hawaii has spawned major research programs. Several initiated in the 1970s and 1980s continue today and now feature over thirty years of continuous observation and data collection. Most studies are multi-year programs exploring larger research questions in stages.

Research is conducted by professional biologists, graduate students, and experienced local researchers, often funded by individuals, non-governmental organizations and charitable foundations.

Individual Identification

What you may see: Research boat maneuvering behind whales. If group is large, or whales are not showing their flukes often, this could continue for hours.

Why? To take identification (ID) photos of individual whales. Each whale is given an ID number and some are even named.

How? Individual humpbacks have unique black-and-white pigment patterns on the underside of their tail flukes. A photograph of these markings provides a permanent ID record of an individual.

What for? ID photos and records of repeat sightings of individuals are the basis of most whale studies today (e.g. for population estimates, local and migratory movement patterns, and behavior studies).

Determining Sex

BILL SCOTT

What you may see: Diver in water; or boat rushing to a breach site then researchers using dip-nets; or boat paralleling a whale to shoot a crossbow dart.

Why? To determine if a whale is male or female.

How? By three techniques: (1) sex-specific behavior (e.g. singers are males, whales with calves are females); (2) arrangement and shape of genital area different from male to female (underwater photo); (3) genetic sex determination from skin sample (sloughed or biopsy).

What for? Knowing the sex of an individual is essential to interpreting behavior patterns and social organization. Genetic analyses also provide information on how whales are related to each other.

Estimating Age

What you may see: Helicopter hovering above a research boat; or boat repeatedly maneuvering to be directly behind whales.

Why? To estimate the age or age class (young, juvenile, adult) of whales.

How? By measuring the size of the whale or some part of it. Photos are taken from the air, surface, or underwater, and size is calculated by photogrammetric comparison. One method is measuring tail flukes (the larger the tail, the larger the whale).

What for? Age data, even relative age estimates (i.e. small, medium, and large whales) are important for the interpretation of social behavior.

Recording Whale Sounds

What you may see: Research boat stationary, engine off, for long periods, occasionally repositioning after a whale surfaces. Or a boat running well ahead of whales stopping, deploying a hydrophone, then remaining stationary as the animals approach.

Why? To record whale songs and social sounds.

How? Sound recordings are made using a hydrophone hanging off the side of the stationary research boat and connected to a recorder.

What for? Sound is a primary sense of whales and is therefore a key to any study of social behavior.

The Research Process

To appreciate the nature of the material in this book requires a few words about the research process. First, it *is* a process — a journey. Researchers begin by knowing little about a topic. In fact, we may have just discovered it exists! Then the scientific work begins, and over time we get closer and closer to an accurate description or understanding of its nature.

During this process we get into the neighborhood of answers. For example, to a question such as "Why do whales breach?" our response would start with field observations like the following:

- Both sexes and all ages of whales breach.
- They breach on breeding grounds and on feeding grounds.
- They breach when alone and in groups.
- They can breach once or many times in succession.
- Whales often breach when they go from calm to windy water.

It can take a long time to answer what seem like the simplest questions about whales. Researchers need to find ways of observing the behavior, develop ideas based on these observations, then test them through scientific studies.

These observations provide us with the context in which they breach. But why do they breach? That we still don't know. The best current guess, considering the observations above, is that it's plain exuberance.

The main point here is that the quality of the answer to any question about whales depends entirely on where the question occurs on the research journey. If near the beginning, the answers researchers supply should be fairly vague, filled with words like initial, preliminary, speculative, or hypothetical. Accept them, because they are likely the best answers we have at the time, but don't take them too much to heart. They may ultimately be proven correct, only partially correct, or even completely wrong! If, on the other hand, the question is asked farther along in the process, with multiple studies completed over a number of years, ideas tested through the scientific process, and with different researchers coming up with the same conclusion, then it means we are getting closer to a definitive answer. With whales, in general, we are fairly early on in the journey.

Humpback Whales

Scientific Name: *Megaptera novaeangliae* (literally, big-winged New Englander). Their common name arose from the arching of their back when diving.

Classification: Humpback whales are one of fifteen species of baleen whales (Mysticeti), divided into four taxonomic families: Eschrichtiidae (gray whales), Balaenidae (right whales), Neobalaenidae (pygmy right whales) and Balaenopteridae (blue, finback, sei, Bryde's, minke, and humpback whales).

Identifying Features: Humpbacks are gray to black with a humplike to sickle-shaped dorsal fin. They have unique, long (15-ft/5-m) black-and-white flippers, distinctive bumps on top of the head, and black-and-white pigment patterns on the underside of the tail flukes.

Size and Weight: Adult, 40–45 feet (12–14 m) and 25–35 tons (estimated). Adult female is larger than male. Newborn calf is 10–15 feet (3–4.5 m) and a yearling is 25–30 feet (8–10 m).

Distribution: Cosmopolitan (worldwide).

Migrations: Migrate annually from high-latitude summer feeding grounds to subtropical or tropical winter breeding grounds.

Food: Larger zooplankton (krill) and a variety of herring-sized fish.

Reproduction: On average one calf every two years.

Life Span: Estimates of 40–80+ years.

Status: On "endangered" lists and protected worldwide, but many populations are recovering. Estimates of numbers: Hawaii 10,000, North Pacific 20,000, world 100,000+.

Humpback whales are easily distinguishable from other large whales by their long black-and-white flippers and knobby heads.

Whales!

Quick Info

What kind of whales are they?

Almost without exception, the whales in Hawaiian waters in winter are humpback whales. Other large whales such as right whales or finbacks are sighted very rarely. A variety of smaller dolphins and other toothed whales live in the area year-round.

What are the humpback whales doing out there?

Hawaiian waters are a breeding ground for humpback whales. So, during the winter, humpbacks migrate to Hawaii to mate and give birth.

Was there ever whaling in Hawaii?

There is no record of commercial whaling in Hawaii. However, during the 1800s, Hawaii (including Lahaina on Maui) was a popular location for whaling ships to spend the winter while waiting for the season to hunt sperm whales in northern seas.

How have we learned about whales?

Our knowledge of whales has come in two distinct phases: (1) studies of dead whales from the whaling industry, mostly ending in the 1960s; and (2) studies of living whales at sea, which began in the 1970s.

How much do we know about whales?

Our scientific understanding of whales is relatively young, with many basic questions still to be answered. However, since the 1970s we have learned more about living whales than in all the previous years combined.

Social Groups
on the Breeding Grounds

Surface Active Group
A surface active group consists of multiple males following a single female (presumably in estrus). Male interaction is predominantly competitive as the female's escort defends his position against challengers.

Singer
A singer is an adult male, usually alone, but at times with another male or female (which may have a calf). He may sing while stationary or traveling.

Joiner
A joiner is a non-singing male that approaches and joins a singer. The singing usually stops as they interact. The whales often split up after a few minutes, but may travel off together.

Surface Active Group (with calf)
Later in the breeding season, the female involved in a surface active group often has a newborn calf by her side. Juveniles are commonly found at the periphery of these groups.

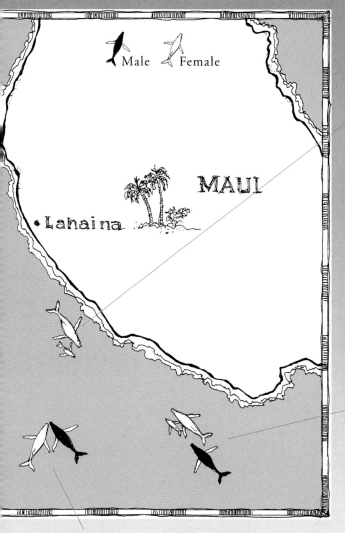

Male Female

MAUI

• Lahaina

Mother/Calf
Mother/calf pairs
may be stationary
(resting) or traveling.
They are often found
in nearshore shallows
and do not mix with
other mother/-calf
pairs. At times a
mother is accompanied
by her yearling, and
occasionally by both
newborn and yearling.

Mother/Calf and Escort
Most mother/calf pairs
are escorted by a male.
The male stays close to
the female and defends
his position against other
males. The female may
accept the male's company
or, at other times, flee.

Female/Male Pair
Adult female/male pairs are common in the first
half of the winter season. Often stationary, they
stay close together, remaining submerged for
15–20+ minutes at a time. The male defends his
position against other males.

*Not shown in the diagram
are lone whales (usually males
traveling to join other whales),
or groups of juveniles.*

Chapter 2

'Hawaiian' Humpbacks

In Hawaii, the first sighting of a humpback whale in the fall is an event. It is usually spotted by a snorkeling boat or fisherman (typically in September or October), and it makes the local newspapers. . . . They're back. The progression of events that comprises the breeding season of humpbacks in Hawaii begins.

The Hawaiian Islands are the focal point for whales that have migrated thousands of miles across open ocean. They swing around the islands, most lingering just weeks in the relative shallows (and increasing social density dramatically), then head back towards their feeding grounds.

It is therefore unlikely the whales you see on one day are the same individuals as the day before. The whale situation in Hawaii is very dynamic, with a virtual parade of individual whales through the region. In addition, the predominant social groups (determined by age, sex, and reproductive stage) change as the season progresses.

What are they doing here? Where do they come from? When are they present? Where are the best places to see them? This chapter answers some of these basic questions about the whales we see in Hawaii. And it sets the stage for the more complex question asked by researchers — why do they behave the way they do?

Hawaii — A Migratory Destination

Worldwide, humpback whales migrate annually between food-rich, cold-water summer feeding grounds and subtropical winter grounds where they breed and give birth. There are eleven populations of humpbacks throughout the world's oceans, each with traditional feeding and breeding grounds. Hawaii is one of these breeding grounds.

The humpback whale migratory pathways are typically between higher and lower latitudes along either side of the continents in both the northern and southern hemispheres. There are exceptions, as a humpback whale population off Oman in the Indian Ocean appears not to migrate at all, and Hawaii, needless to say, is in the middle of the largest ocean in the world.

Why Migrate?

Scientists do not yet understand why humpback whales make this annual migration thousands of miles away from their food supply. The shortest distance from Hawaii to Alaska is about 2,700 miles (4,400 km) one way. Humpbacks make a huge seasonal shift, from a context of feeding, resting, and net energy gain, to one of significant energy

Humpback whales make a huge seasonal shift in behavior, from summer feeding and net energy gain (*left*), to winter fasting and major energy expenditure (*right*).

expenditure involving traveling, fasting, birthing, nursing, and mating.

Two key environmental conditions are the same for humpback whale winter assembly areas worldwide: relatively warm water and shallow depth. The temperature of the water in North Pacific breeding grounds ranges from approximately 66–77°F (19–25°C), compared to feeding-ground temperatures of 46–57°F (8–14°C). Breeding grounds are typically situated on shallow banks several hundreds of feet deep, whereas surrounding waters (as well as waters in the feeding grounds) may be thousands of feet deep.

Presumably, these conditions improve the chances of successful reproduction, and perhaps especially serve the needs of mothers with newborn calves. Exactly how these environmental conditions are important to breeding whales is not yet known, although they probably meet both physiological (energetic) and behavioral needs.

Humpback whales that feed in widely separated regions in summer concentrate and mix during the winter assembly. This gathering may therefore promote genetic mixing and diversity, which may be another function of migrations. The concentration of whales on the breeding grounds also makes it easier for them to find each other.

North Pacific Humpback Whale Migrations

North Pacific humpback whales leave summer feeding grounds around the Pacific Rim (*light shading*) and migrate to three main winter assembly areas in subtropical and tropical waters (*dark shading*).

Humpback whales spend the summer in cold-water feeding grounds around the North Pacific Rim, from California to northern Japan. In late fall and early winter, most leave their summer grounds and migrate to subtropical breeding grounds. In the North Pacific, there are three general regions where humpbacks assemble in the winter: (1) in the eastern North Pacific from Mexico southwards as far as Costa Rica; (2) in the central North Pacific around the main Hawaiian Islands; and (3) in the western North Pacific from southern Japan to Taiwan and the northern Philippines.

Humpback whales on specific feeding grounds are more likely to migrate to one breeding ground over another. Migratory destinations have been determined with three techniques: (1) the use of Discovery tags in the whaling era (metal darts shot into whales and recovered at a later date and location, when the whale was killed and rendered); (2) resightings of photo-identified individual whales; and (3) observations of satellite-tagged whales.

Researchers have learned that:

- Humpback whales that feed from Northern California to Vancouver Island in the summer are almost always found in Mexican and Central American breeding grounds in the winter.

- Humpbacks that feed from Vancouver Island to Alaska in summer are often found in Hawaii in winter, although some migrate to Mexico.

- Humpbacks that feed in the Bering Sea, along the western Aleutian Islands, and along the Russian coast are more likely to be found in the Asian wintering areas.

However, there are marked exceptions to these generalities. Some whales head to breeding areas far distant from that of their summer neighbors. Moreover, individuals have been identified in one breeding ground one year and in another the next! That is, for instance, in Mexico one winter and in Hawaii another winter, or in Japan one year and in Hawaii another year.

It took one whale a maximum of 39 days to migrate between SE Alaska and Hawaii (determined by photo-identification in both locations).

Gabriele et al. 1996

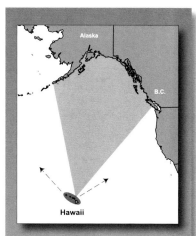

Where Are the 'Hawaiian' Humpbacks in Summer?

Perhaps the best way of thinking about the summer grounds of Hawaiian humpbacks is to picture a piece of pie with the point on Hawaii.

Most humpbacks seen in Hawaii migrate to summer feeding grounds in Alaska and British Columbia (BC). Numerous individual whales have been photo-identified in both locations, and whales satellite-tagged in Hawaii migrated directly to northern BC and southeast Alaskan waters.

It is, however, important to emphasize that any single humpback seen in Hawaii could potentially spend the summer in just about any location around the Pacific Rim. Indeed, one whale satellite-tagged in Hawaii spent the summer in Russian waters.

'Missing' Whales?

Some mature females apparently do not make the entire migration to the breeding grounds each year, presumably due to the high energy costs of migration and reproduction. There is an ongoing discussion among researchers about females 'missing' from the breeding grounds, and it is generally agreed that far more males than females make the migration. Possible reasons include some females taking a 'rest year,' and some females becoming pregnant en route and returning to the feeding grounds instead of continuing to Hawaii.

Currently there is more speculation than hard data on this subject. For example, research on the number, sex, and identity of whales that remain off Alaska during winter does not show that females are in the majority, as might be expected if males are in the majority in Hawaii. So the question of exactly where the 'missing' females are remains open.

Biopsy sampling during the migrations of humpback whales along the east coast of Australia (to and from South Pacific breeding grounds) revealed a sex ratio of 2.4 males to every 1 female.

Brown et al.
1995

JIM DARLING

Humpback whales worldwide seek out warm, relatively shallow waters for winter breeding grounds. Hawaii is one such location.

Breeding And Nursery Grounds

Geography or Behavior?

It's convenient to say that humpback whales come to Hawaii to breed and give birth, but that's not strictly true. Reproductive activities begin, and some births occur, before the whales reach Hawaii. In fact, some behavior patterns related to breeding activity, such as singing, begin as early as late fall and before the whales leave their summer feeding grounds. It is apparent that reproductive behavior occurs throughout the southern migration, peaks during the winter assembly in Hawaii, and then continues to some extent on the northern migration back to feeding grounds. For this reason, the geographic boundaries of where breeding behavior occurs (that is, the "breeding grounds") are not easily defined.

Where are the Whales in Hawaii?

Humpback whales are most abundant in a specific habitat in the Hawaiian Islands — they prefer the 'shallow' banks less than 600 feet (180 m) deep that encircle, or in some cases connect, islands. This habitat is in contrast to the deep-water channels up to 6,000 feet (1,900 m) deep and the ocean basin that surround these islands. Therefore, in general, the greater the extent of the shallow banks, the more abundant the whales. However, the whales regularly cross the deep inter-island channels to move between islands.

During aerial surveys, the majority of whales (74%) were found in water of less than about 100 fathoms (600 ft).

Mobley et al.
1994

Whales are found throughout the main Hawaiian Islands in winter, with higher concentrations in certain locations *(dark shading).*

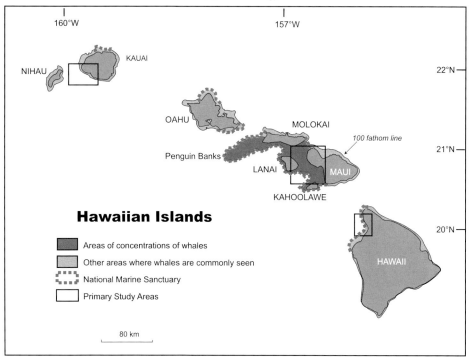

Hawaiian Islands

- Areas of concentrations of whales
- Other areas where whales are commonly seen
- National Marine Sanctuary
- Primary Study Areas

80 km

Blows are easy to spot from the West Maui shoreline in late afternoon and evening as the sun sets behind the island of Lanai.

When Is The Best Time To See Whales?

Humpbacks are winter visitors to Hawaii. They are most abundant from mid-December through early April, with peak numbers in February and March. Humpbacks have been seen as early as September and as late as June, but sightings before November or after May are rare.

The most common whale groupings vary over the course of the season. That is, whale watchers in January are likely to see different types of groups than whale watchers in March. This is partly due to staggered arrival and departure times of whales based on their age, sex, and reproductive stage.

Our knowledge of the order of the migration (and the arrival and departure from the breeding grounds) comes primarily from studies conducted during whaling operations in different parts of the world. It was discovered that if whaling occurred throughout an entire season on humpback breeding grounds, then the status of the whales caught changed (in terms of age, sex, and reproductive stage). These studies

The type of whale group most likely to be seen on the breeding grounds changes as the season progresses due to migratory order and reproductive status. For example, in the early season, adult male/female pairs (*above*) are very common; later, mothers with a calf and male escort (*below*) predominate.

suggest the migratory order to and from the breeding grounds as follows, with a degree of overlap among the groups.

Arrival Order	Departure Order
1st Females with yearling	1st Mature females**
2nd Immature whales	2nd Immature whales
3rd Mature (resting*) females	3rd Mature males
4th Mature males	4th New mothers
5th Females in late pregnancy	

* Ovaries and mammary glands showed no signs of recent activity.
**Newly pregnant or in a rest year.

This sequence found by whalers (mostly in the southern hemisphere) is somewhat confirmed by observations in Hawaii. Juveniles and adult pairs (presumably male/female) without a calf are common in December, January, and early February; the numbers of new mothers with a calf increases after February 1 and through March; and mothers with newborn calves are the last to depart in April and May. At the peak of the season, all age, sex, and reproductive categories are present.

A procession of humpback whales passes through the Hawaiian Islands in winter, most lingering in the relatively shallow waters for several weeks.

How Long Does Any Individual Whale Stay In Hawaii?

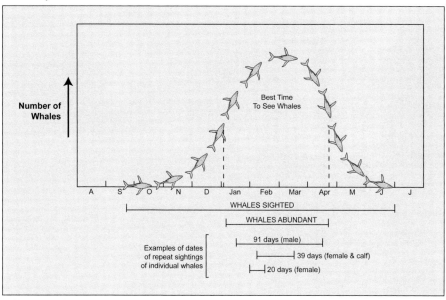

Humpback whales are abundant in Hawaii between December and April, with peak numbers in February and March. Most individual whales stay in Hawaii for relatively short periods (weeks), but some males stay much longer (months).

So far, we have a picture for when whales are most abundant and when different age, sex, and reproductive classes may arrive and depart. In addition, studies suggest that most individual whales do not spend the whole season in Hawaii, and in fact are present for relatively short periods of the overall humpback season.

This insight comes primarily from the number of days or weeks between resightings of photo-identified individuals. When researchers compare all the identification pictures taken in one season, they find within-year

*There is,
so to speak, a
marching column
in the migration
of whales.*

Nishiwaki
1962

Repeat sightings of individual whales (identified by photographs of the permanent skin pigment patterns on the underside of the flukes) allow estimates of the length of their stay in Hawaii.

matches — whales seen more than once. For example, Whale #971 may have been seen on February 5, February 12, and March 15, with a total time between first and last sightings of thirty-nine days *(see chart on page 43)*.

These analyses suggest that most individual whales arrive, spend about a month to six weeks in Hawaii, then leave just as other individuals arrive in succession, and so on. There is, however, a possible exception to this pattern — some males may spend a significantly longer time in the region than other males and females. This suggestion is supported by three pieces of information. (1) All whales of known sex present over more than eight weeks are males. (2) The longest periods of repeat sightings of males are about three months, or the length of the peak season. (3) There are several examples of the same individual males repeating their long stays from year to year. In contrast, the longest period between repeat sightings of females is about seven weeks *(see chart on page 43)*.

The weak point in these analyses is that the study areas where the photo-identifications are taken are small relative to the whole Hawaiian range *(see map on page 39)*. Therefore, it is possible that individuals not seen anymore and presumed to have returned to the feeding grounds could simply be outside the study area but still present in the Islands. The reason researchers don't think this is the case is that several different studies have arrived at the same conclusion for individual length of stay — for instance, satellite tags have indicated whales tagged in Hawaii early in the season may return to the feeding areas before most whales even reach Hawaii, and whales (thought to be a succession of different individuals) are seen on the feeding grounds throughout the winter.

Another study used a mathematical model based on the expected number of repeat sightings of individuals to estimate population size. It found more repeat sightings than expected for a small sub-population of the whales. Apparently, these individuals remained in the area for longer than average (creating a greater chance of them being resighted). The researchers speculated that this subgroup may be mature and perhaps dominant males. These whales may remain longer to maximize opportunities to mate, although this has yet to be proven.

Although whales were present off Maui over five months or more, 88% of repeat sightings of individuals were within six weeks, and the majority within two weeks. All 17 whales (of known sex) resighted over more than six weeks were males.

Darling
1983

The mean 'residence' time for 16 satellite-tagged whales in Hawaii is 13.4 days, but arrival time (in Hawaii) is unknown.

Mate et al.
2007

JIM DARLING

During their stay in the region, individual whales circulate freely between the main Hawaiian Islands.

Whale Movements Within The Hawaiian Islands

Studies based on photo-identification and satellite-tagging now suggest that the norm for all social classes of whales is to circulate throughout the main Hawaiian Island chain, with no animals remaining in one specific area for very long.

One early study proposed a more organized movement where whales entered the Hawaiian chain at the southern end of the Big Island (Hawaii) and generally moved through the region southeast to north-west, eventually leaving from Kauai. This was based on whale counts in the 1980s that seemed to indicate a shift in highest whale densities in this direction as the winter season progressed. However, photo-identified whales were subsequently found moving in the reverse direction (northwest to southeast), from Maui to the Big Island, and Kauai to the Big Island, indicating a one-way flow was not an accurate picture. More recently, satellite tags have revealed whales circulating (seemingly at random) throughout the main island chain. This satellite-tracking study also noted that Kauai may be a northward migration departure point. Hence, there remains some speculation that individuals may make a final move to the northwest before departing.

Nine whales moved one way from Hawaii to Kauai and six moved the reverse direction from Kauai to Hawaii, i.e., no directional trend. The shortest inter-island movement time was eight days.

Cerchio et al.
1998

This map shows the results of three studies of whale movements within Hawaii. Studies A and B are based on photo-identification matches, study C is a satellite-tag track. Study A shows short-term moves back and forth between the Big Island (Hawaii) and Maui; B shows within-season travels from the Big Island to Kauai and the reverse; and C (based on a satellite-tag track) shows one tagged whale that traveled extensivey in a 10-day period.

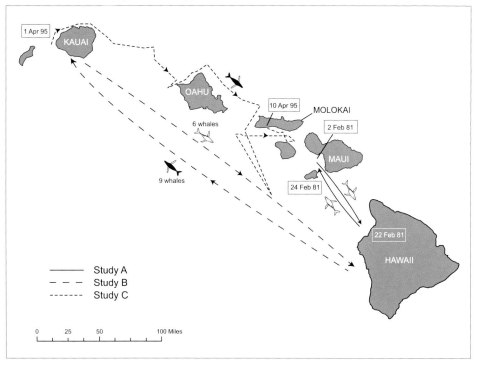

Is There Location-Specific Activity In The Islands?

There is a twofold picture emerging — no social/behavioral boundaries within the main Hawaiian Islands and high mobility throughout the islands by all social groups (possibly some more than others). However, despite this mounting evidence, some researchers continue to speculate that the whales behave differently in different places.

There was an early (1980s) suggestion that some degree of segregation occurs between whales wintering off different islands — that is, different individuals migrate to different islands. This idea is certainly no longer viable. However, the notion persists that the predominant social groups and related behavior patterns may vary to some extent among certain locations. Recently, one research group suggested that the distribution of females in Hawaiian waters may depend on

A humpback leaps from the water just yards off a West Maui shore.

reproductive status, with females more likely to be accompanied by calves off Maui than off the Big Island of Hawaii.

The idea that whales are more likely to be engaged in a type of activity in one location versus another has not been proven. If it does occur, one might expect it to be related to specific habitat conditions (i.e. physical attributes of an area such as shallowness) regardless of where these are rather than to specific geographic locations.

One whale, tracked by satellite tag, traveled at least 820 km in ten days (a mean of 80 km/day) through the coastal waters of five of the Hawaiian Islands: Kauai, Oahu, Molokai, and through Penguin Bank and the Kalohi Channel between Molokai, Maui, and Lanai.

Mate et al.
1998

A mother rests in relative shallows just outside Lahaina harbor, while her calf peeks above the surface.

The clearest case of habitat preference is that mothers with young calves are consistently found in shallower, more in-shore waters than most of the population *(see Chapter 6)*. They are not, however, found only in shallow waters or in one region within the islands, so researchers have not been able to define specific nursery areas or conditions. In fact, mothers with calves move throughout the island chain, and are regularly sighted on Penguin Bank *(see map on page 39)*, which has some of the roughest off-shore water in the area.

Humpback whales worldwide seek out warm, relatively shallow waters in winter for mating and birth. Hawaii is the largest breeding ground for this species in the North Pacific, with many of the whales migrating from feeding grounds along the northwest coast of North America. From December through April, humpbacks are abundant around the main Hawaiian Islands, but most individual whales are present for just a small portion of the overall season. There is constant movement and circulation of individuals throughout the island chain, probably dictated by social interactions. Now, the next question for researchers is, why do they behave this way?

'Hawaiian' Humpbacks

Quick Info

Why are the whales in Hawaii?

Humpback whales migrate to Hawaii to mate and give birth. They make long migrations between colder summer feeding grounds and subtropical winter breeding areas. Hawaii is the largest breeding ground for humpbacks in the North Pacific.

Why migrate?

Scientists do not really understand why the whales migrate thousands of miles from their feeding grounds each year. It is apparent that environmental conditions of relatively warm water and comparatively shallow ocean depths (as in Hawaii) are important to reproductive success in humpback whales.

Where do they come from?

Humpback whales that spend the summer feeding along the coastline from Vancouver Island to Alaska are most likely to migrate to Hawaii in winter.

Do all humpback whales migrate each year?

There is evidence that not all mature females make the migration, or at least the entire migration, each year. It is thought that females in a resting (non-reproductive) year, or those that become pregnant en route, may not show up on the breeding grounds.

When is the best time to see humpbacks in Hawaii?

Humpback whales are common in Hawaii from December through April, with peak abundance in February and March.

Where is the best location to see whales in Hawaii?

Humpback whales can be sighted around all the main Hawaiian Islands. The highest densities of whales are within the Four Island Group of Maui, Molokai, Lanai, and Kahoolawe, and on Penguin Bank off the northwestern tip of Molokai. Whales are a little less concentrated but still plentiful off the Kona coast of Hawaii and around Kauai.

How long does an individual whale stay in Hawaii?

Most individual whales stay for short periods of time (several weeks) relative to the overall five- to six-month season, with other individuals arriving in succession as they leave. Some individual males may stay on the breeding grounds for most of the season.

How do whales move locally and use the area?

Individual whales appear to circulate freely around all the main Hawaiian Islands, and rarely stay in a specific location for any length of time.

Chapter 3

Breeding Season

Why do whales behave like they do in Hawaii? Why do they form the kinds of groups we see, such as mothers with newborn calves accompanied by a male escort, or groups of multiple males chasing one female? Why do they sing, and fight, and cooperate? The answers all lie, ultimately, in the female humpback whale's biology.

During the winter, a portion of female humpbacks come into relatively brief periods of heightened sexual receptivity called estrus (known as "heat" in domestic animals). Humpbacks are seasonally polyestrus, undergoing several estrus cycles during a single winter season until successfully pregnant.

Males organize and behave to take advantage of this pattern of female availability and receptiveness. The force behind male behavior on the breeding grounds is not complicated — the urge to mate with as many females as possible — and, as in most mammal societies, their role in reproduction is fleeting.

For females, on the other hand, successful mating leads to a two-year time and energy commitment. The female must nourish the fetus for a year, then give birth, then support the newborn for up to another year. Her success depends on sufficient, and efficient, energy budgeting. It's serious business, and her behavior reflects this.

A humpback female (*center*) juggles newborn care and male attention during the breeding season.

Seasonal Cycles Of Humpback Whales

There are three interrelated cycles that determine the behavior of the female — and hence the male — humpback whale.

- A humpback's year is divided between a feeding season in the summer (includes spring, summer, fall) and a breeding season in winter. In the high latitudes, humpback food (krill and small fish) is abundant in the summer season, but by comparison rare in winter. The humpbacks therefore feed continually when food is available, and shift to mating and birthing when it is not. There is, apparently, an advantage to carrying out the latter in warmer waters, so they migrate.

- Humpback whales have a specific reproductive cycle with the same components as all mammals: mating, gestation, birth, and nurturing young. The time between these points in the cycle, as well as the timing and duration of events, is determined by evolutionary and ecological forces. The typical reproductive cycle of a mature humpback is: mating in winter, a year's gestation, birth of one baby during the following (second) winter, a year's care of the baby prior to weaning, then separation in the third winter followed by mating again.

- Within this general pattern, individual females have their own cycles, with estrus occurring at different times and frequencies dependent on condition and age. In North Pacific humpback whales, females collectively come into estrus over the six winter months, but any individual female may be receptive for just a short period during that season or may come into estrus several times if she does not become pregnant the first time. (The sexual cycles of males, with varying production of sperm, tend to reflect the timing of the female breeding season.)

Vital Statistics

Age of maturity
May vary by region; range 4–15 years

Birth rate
Average 1 calf every 2 to 3 years; annual birth possible

Gestation
11–11.5 months

Lactation 10 months

Estrus
Peak 3–5 winter months
Recurrence Seasonally poly-estrus (repeated cycles if no pregnancy)
Duration of one cycle
Unknown
Postpartum
Common, but odds of conception low

Spermatogenesis
Peak during winter months

Operational sex ratio on breeding grounds
2 to 3 males to 1 female

The male in the foreground is escorting or guarding
this stationary female, who is likely in or near estrus.

Underwater observation and photography of mothers with newborn calves have advanced our understanding of humpback whale reproductive behavior. (Federal and state permits are required to swim with whales in Hawaii.)

How Have We Learned About Humpback Reproductive Cycles?

Beyond our noticing when females have young calves (versus older calves or yearlings), our understanding of humpback reproduction has been pieced together from three sources:

- Examination of the reproductive organs of dead whales. Large-scale whaling operations in the first half of the 1900s led to tens of thousands of whales being examined. The resulting information has provided much of the framework of humpback reproductive biology.

- Records of birth histories of individual females seen and photo-identified annually. In some cases, a particular female was photo-identified first as a calf, and then sighted each year until she had her own first calf, providing information on age of sexual maturity.

- Male behavior patterns that suggest females are in or near estrus. Simply, the more males and the greater the activity levels around a female, the more likely she is in estrus (or so we assume).

The photo-identification of mothers (such as this one with a tiny newborn calf at her side) and repeat sightings over many years provide insight into birth rates.

JIM DARLING

The best way of estimating age of sexual maturity of a living whale is establishing when a female of known age has her first calf. This is achieved by first photo-identifying females when just a calf and then annually until they produce their first offspring.

Sexual Maturity And Birth Rate

Our understanding of the onset of sexual maturity (estimated by the age a female has her first calf), and then birth rate, is incomplete. Research has provided a range of age of maturity and the main birth patterns, but there remain some key questions to be resolved.

As mentioned above, the two means of estimating age of sexual maturity are from data on whaled specimens and from analyses of living females identified since birth who later produced their own calf. The whaling studies (primarily from the southern hemisphere) estimated age of sexual maturity at 4–6 years based on examination of ovaries. A North Atlantic research project on living whales indicated that the humpbacks have their first calf from 5–7 years of age, which appears to agree with the whaling studies. However, in some contrast to this, a similar study in Alaska indicates that humpbacks there do not have a first calf until 8–16 years, twice the age of the North Atlantic sample! (Further, Alaskan researchers raise questions about the method of age determination in the whaling studies, suggesting it could be off by half.)

So, the available information suggests that humpback females in the North Pacific are twice as old as those in the North Atlantic before having a first calf. This is presently a challenge for researchers, who must explain why age of maturity would differ to this degree. It may be the result of a different ecology between oceans or differing impacts on the populations from whaling.

Once a female has reached sexual maturity, the average birth rate is one calf every two to three years. This rate varies from one female to another and within the same individual over time. Most females are on a two-year cycle with mating one year, birth the next, and so on. Some females, by choice or circumstance, have a resting year in the sequence so that their birth rate may be once every three years.

This pattern seems to make sense considering the energy cost of pregnancy and nursing the calf. It would appear the optimum situation for a mother is not to have both occurring simultaneously. Think of a 10–12 month gestation (nutrition of the fetus) period overlapping the same period as lactation (production of milk for the newborn). This is not likely to favor the strongest and healthiest offspring.

Female humpback whales of known age in the Gulf of Maine produced first observed calves at ages ranging from 5–7.

Clapham
1992

The age distribution of eleven mothers with their first calf in southeastern Alaska was 8–16 years (mean 11.8 years).

Gabriele et al.
2007

Groups of males chasing and aggressively competing for access to a female suggests she is in estrus.

Mating Time

Estrus: Occurrence, Recurrence, and Duration

Recall that the humpback whale food supply is primarily available in summer months, which has led to non-feeding, reproductive behavior occurring in winter. Studies during the whaling era indicated that the peak of the sexual cycle in humpback whales in general occurs during the three-to-five winter months. In the North Pacific, one study on sexual cycles based on whales hunted in Japan in the 1950s and 60s determined the peak of female estrus to be in February. This timing matches well with the peak abundance of whales and male engagement with females in Hawaii *(see chart on page 68)*.

Again, however, it may not be quite this clear cut. Several studies in other locations, also based on examination of ovaries, indicate that successful pregnancies can occur well out of synchronization with the majority. One examination of humpback whale fetuses in the North Pacific suggests that successful mating can occur in eleven or even twelve months of the year, with two apparent peaks, one in the February–April period and the other in September! This potentially wide range of timing of mating, conception, and subsequent birth has not been substantiated by recent studies and is rarely emphasized in the literature. However, occasional sightings of humpbacks in Hawaii

Estrus Cycles

Estrus is the period of sexual receptivity in female mammals commonly known as "heat" in domestic animals. It is often affected by seasons, and more specifically by the hours of daylight, which govern the release of key hormones. During estrus, ovulation — the production of eggs — occurs, and pregnancy will likely result from mating activity. These hormones greatly affect behavior. The critical question is timing: how often does the cycle of estrus then anestrus (no estrus) repeat itself, and how long does the estrus period of maximum receptivity last? Virtually nothing is known about this subject in baleen whales. However, an example from domestic sheep (curiously enough) provides some insight into the nature of the cycle.

Most female sheep (ewes) are seasonally polyestrus [yes, the same phrase used to describe humpback whales] *and short-day breeders* [sexually active in fall or winter, also likely the case for humpback whales]. *They will begin to exhibit estrus when the length of day begins decreasing. They* [the sheep] *will come into heat every 16–17 days, which lasts 1–2 days, until they are bred or return to anestrus. The natural time for sheep to breed in the northern hemisphere is in the fall, October or November. When mature ewes are in heat, they will seek out the ram and stand still for him to mount them. Sometimes they wag their tails vigorously or may nuzzle the ram.*

— Susan Schoenian

Sheep may seem a distant subject to whales, but in fact they are not. The extant (currently living) mammals most closely related (genetically) to whales are the Artiodactyls — even-toed ungulates (hoofed animals) that include sheep.

The peak of ovulation (in humpbacks whaled in Okinawa, Japan) occurred between the end of January and the end of February.

Nishiwaki
1959

in September and October (purposes unknown), and large calves present early in the winter season (January–February), clearly born weeks or even months earlier, make it prudent not to rule out this possibility.

As mentioned earlier, humpback females come into estrus and ovulate seasonally, and during that season may have several cycles. The duration of a single humpback estrus period, or time between multiple cycles, is not known. Our knowledge of this is so scant that one observation in Hawaii of the same female leading competitive groups of males on both February 1 and 6 (1980) may be the best (however circumstantial) indication that estrus extended over a six-day period.

The figure below is based on records of multiple males competing over a single female (presumably in estrus). The male focus on females without calves peaks several weeks before similar behavior around mothers with calves. This analysis suggests estrus in humpback whales occurs from December to April, with a peak in February–March.

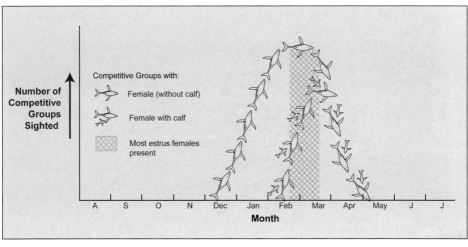

A mother with her newborn calf (*center*) is pursued by several males. This type of group peaks in March and suggests the mother is in postpartum (shortly after birth) estrus.

Male Behavior Indicates Female Estrus

Our only insight into the timing and duration of estrus for humpback whales specifically in Hawaiian waters (where there is no data from whaling) are behavioral observations of extreme male interest in, and competition over, females. In practice, this means researchers record when multiple males are seen competing for a female and make an assumption that this activity means the female is in estrus.

In Hawaii, this competitive behavior has been documented from December

Based on the occurrence and relative numbers of surface active groups, the most estrus females without a calf occurred through February and March, several weeks earlier than the peak number of estrus females with a young calf.

Darling
1983

Competitive groups around a female without calf were most frequent from 9 February to 19 March, whereas groups around a female with a calf peaked from 19 February to 1 April. The overlap in these dates is the height of breeding activity.

Gabriele
1992

to May, suggesting estrus females are present in Hawaii over these six months. These groups are most common from mid-January to mid-April. The peak occurrence of males following females without a calf occurs in February and March, which is several weeks earlier than the peak of males pursuing females with a young calf.

This height of (presumed) estrus activity correlates well with the timing of other behavioral indicators such as peak transience of whales in groups (or the shortest period that males stay in one group), aggressive encounters, and singing. (It also correlates well with dates of peak ovulations estimated from data from hunted whales.)

This male escort is chasing a female (with calf) at high speed and lifting her flukes with his head. Males have been observed to rush in directly under a female's tail stock (and genital area) then back off to typical escort position — perhaps checking her state of estrus?

JIM DARLING

How Do Males Know a Female Is Ready to Mate?

We do not know how male whales determine a female is ready to mate. In land mammals, females release scents, give visual clues such as swelling of sexual organs, or change behavior to make themselves available to, or actively pursue, males. In whales we do not know what role, if any, smell (or taste) may play as little is known about these senses in baleen whales. It seems unlikely that visual clues are important in the ocean, as a male virtually has to run into a female to see her! So, for humpbacks, the third mammalian possibility, of females changing their behavior and making sure males find them, may be a large part of the answer.

What We See And Why

It is interesting (and important) to explore the cause of much of the whale action seen in Hawaiian waters.

The most exciting whale behavior for whale watchers is groups of males chasing and fighting over a female. The reason this occurs is that the majority of females give birth every two or three years, so many are not available each breeding season — though there are equal numbers of males and females in the population overall. This results in an *operational* sex ratio of two to three males for every female. The males, therefore, compete for the relatively few receptive females.

Another example is that mothers with a newborn calf are usually accompanied by an adult male escort. This grouping exists because the mother undergoes a postpartum estrus, attracting the males.

Also, the very fact that the whale season in Hawaii extends over five or six months (meaning one can see whales December through April) is the result of the spread of estrus times of individual females.

In every case, the behavior of whales in Hawaii is a consequence of the female reproductive cycle.

Groups of agitated males competing for a receptive female make for good whale watching.

Humpback whales behave as they do in Hawaii because it works. The social groups, actions, and interactions occurring lead to successful pregnancies and offspring — otherwise they would not happen. Patterns of female availability and receptiveness are determined by their physiology and are linked to broader ecological factors. In turn, male behavior has evolved in response to these female patterns. Much of the information in the next few chapters describes the behavior that makes humpback whale reproduction successful.

Breeding Season

Quick Info

What ultimately determines whale behavior in Hawaii?

The distribution of sexually receptive females, in time and space, directs male mating strategies and specific behavior.

When is sexual maturity?

The best information to date, derived from when a female of known age has her first calf, suggests age of sexual maturity varies with location and population of humpback whales (range 4–15 years old).

How often do females give birth?

The average birth rate for a humpback whale is one calf every two to three years. However, some females may produce a calf each year for up to four sequential years.

When do female humpbacks come into estrus?

Female humpback whales typically come into estrus during the winter months, with a peak in the North Pacific from January to March. Each individual female comes into estrus for short periods during that time and either becomes pregnant or repeats the cycle.

How do males know a female is in estrus?

We do not know the answer to this question. From studies of land mammals, it's likely the females provide some form of signal, either through a discharge the males can sense and/or by changing their behavior to make themselves available to males.

How do males react to female sexual cycles?

All male behavior patterns on the breeding grounds (including time of arrival and length of stay) are probably governed by the female cycles. For example, there are more mature males than receptive females present on the breeding grounds at any one time, hence male/male competition occurs for the limited females.

Why do males escort females with a newborn calf?

The females come into estrus shortly after giving birth — hence the male attention. Researchers hypothesize that while estrus and ovulation occur at this time, few successful pregnancies result (but then the males do not know this!).

Chapter 4

Mating — The Male Perspective

Mating, needless to say, is a major item on the agenda of whales in Hawaii. Indeed, it is the only item for males. In any mating situation there are reciprocal male and female behavior patterns, as both want to succeed. However, there is conflict between individual males, each attempting to maximize number of matings, and conflict between the males and a female, who needs to make the most of her mating opportunity — meaning mating with a strong (healthy) male while using up as little energy as possible.

The behavioral story revolves around the fact that there are more sexually mature males than receptive females present at any one time — potentially a lot more. This is good for females, but perhaps not so good for males. To mate, a male must first locate a receptive female, then he must outmaneuver (or otherwise come to terms with) other males that are equally interested in (and willing to fight over) her, and then face the issue of whether or not she will accept him as a suitable mate.

The strategies and behavior involved — from singing complex songs, to stunning battles that can leave blood streaming from head, back, or tail, to teamwork that challenges behavioral theory — are the subject of this chapter.

Male behavior on the breeding grounds is often overt. This male, accompanying a female, makes his displeasure clear (with a vigorous display of bubbles from his blowhole) at the approach of another male.

Singing, Escorting, Competing, And (Perhaps) Cooperating

Male humpback whales in Hawaii are found alone, with other males, and in associations and interactions with females. In this chapter, male behavior patterns are divided into two sections:

- Male/male behavior, which includes singing and joining singers — at times forming male pairs, or larger all-male groups.

- Male behavior around a female, which includes:

  (a) Male/female pairs, when a single male escorts an adult female.

  (b) Multiple male/single female interactions that involve males competing, or cooperating, to gain access to the female.

In Hawaii, most male interactions and associations (both with other males and with females) appear short-lived, lasting only minutes to hours. Then the males move on to the next interaction. A 'long' association might have a male paired with a female (with or without a calf) for a day or so. There is one report of a mother/yearling pair that was escorted by the same male over two days. Whereas researchers agree that males orient to any female in estrus, there is less agreement as to the nature of male/male relations. Most of the earlier literature on this subject suggests males either avoid each other or fight. However, more recent studies have indicated that non-agonistic (friendly) male/male interactions are common, and may even lead in some cases to temporary cooperative unions.

*The sex of a
total of 22 joiners
[of singers]
was determined,
14 genetically, eight
by behavior.
All were males.*

Darling and Bérubé
2001

Bulletin: No One Has Actually Seen Mating!

Any discussion of mating behavior must begin with this caveat — there is no documented observation of humpback whale copulation in Hawaiian waters to date. Even with untold thousands of observer hours each season, for more than thirty years, it has not been recorded. (In other species of baleen whales, copulation is commonly observed.) On the other hand, the circumstantial evidence that mating occurs is over-whelming.

This strange situation leaves us guessing as to when and in which behavior pattern or social group copulation actually occurs, what behavior precedes and follows it, or if an individual animal mates once or many times during the season. And, of course, it makes any discussion of mating behavior unavoidably speculative.

Male/Male Behavior

Singing

Male humpback whales sing songs — a complex series of sounds repeated over and over. Singing apparently coincides with the breeding season. Bits of song have (rarely) been recorded in summer, but singing begins in earnest on the fall and early winter feeding grounds, occurs through the migration, likely peaks in the winter assembly, and then falls off in the spring.

Humpback whale song can be heard anytime, anywhere around Hawaii in winter with a hydrophone, or without one virtually anytime one goes swimming and dives beneath the surface along the shoreline. Near a singer underwater, it is about as loud as a home stereo turned up full-blast. In fact, the song is so loud it can be heard emanating from the ocean on a quiet day. Although the amount of singing in a given area may change through the day (and night), singers provide a continual acoustic background to the breeding grounds.

Humpbacks emit sounds in long, predictable patterns ranging over frequencies audible to humans.

**Payne and McVay
1971**

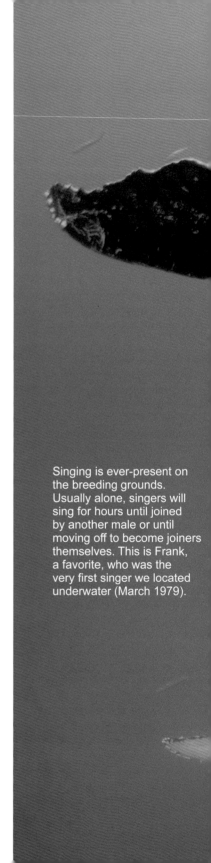

Singing is ever-present on the breeding grounds. Usually alone, singers will sing for hours until joined by another male or until moving off to become joiners themselves. This is Frank, a favorite, who was the very first singer we located underwater (March 1979).

When singing, the whale takes several breaths then dives, leaving a circular slick on the surface. Often, as shown in inset, the singer simply stops 20–40 feet (7–13 m) directly below the slick and at about a 45-degree angle, nose down and tail up.

Here is what is known about singing humpback whales:

- Singing is a male behavior pattern. To date, there has been no record of a female singing.

- Singers are most often lone adult whales. In a minority of encounters, the singer has an adult companion that may be either male or female (at times with calf; that is, the escort accompanying a mother with a calf is singing). There have been a few observations of smaller, juvenile whales near a singer. It is not known at what age males begin singing, but it is presumed to relate to sexual maturity.

- Singers are often stationary (in Hawaiian waters) in what has become known as a singing posture, with tail up and head down at an angle of about forty-five degrees. The tail of the singer is usually about 20–40 feet (7–13 m) beneath the surface. (In some breeding grounds, singers hold this posture with their tail above the surface of the sea.) Whales may also sing while moving around the breeding grounds, as well as during migrations.

- Singing typically continues until: (1) the singer is joined by another whale(s), usually a lone adult male, but occasionally a pair; or (2) the singer stops to join a passing group that includes a female — either a competitive group composed of a female and several males, a male/female pair, or a mother and calf with or without an escort.

The amount of singing increased significantly at night off West Maui.

Au et al.
2000

Bermuda and Whale Song

"Suddenly, I was startled by a loud, low-frequency moan which boomed over the loudspeaker. . . . My imagination soared and I couldn't wait to discover the source."*

— Frank Watlington
Bermuda, April 1952

There is no doubt our species has been aware of humpback songs since the first mariner. However, it was not until the 1950s that the first recordings were made — inadvertently.

Frank Watlington, while manning an early underwater listening station in Bermuda, was among the first to realize the source of these sounds.

Watlington's humpback recordings became the main resource for researchers Roger Payne and Scott McVay, who introduced whale songs to the world in 1971 (in the journal *Science*).

* In Bermuda Zoological Society 1983, from Dietz 1982.

The Song

Song Structure

The humpback whale song is a series of sounds that typically lasts 10–15 minutes and is repeated over and over.

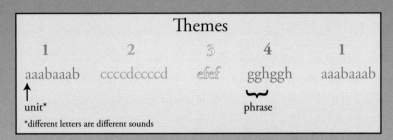

The song consists of several different *themes* (often four to six) sung in a continuous loop. Each theme is composed of sound *units* distinctly arranged as a *phrase*, which is repeated for several minutes. The singer progresses through each of the themes (all with different unit/phrase compositions) until he has worked through the entire song. If the song has four themes the whale will sing Themes 1-2-3-4, usually surface to breathe, then dive and begin Theme 1 again. A song *session* (that is, continuous singing) can last hours.

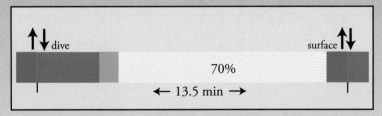

Here the themes (composed as above) are given different colors. All singers in the population follow the same pattern of theme composition and progression. Even the amount of time spent on one theme is similar. During this period (Jan. 2005), about 70 percent of the Hawaii song consisted of Theme 3 (yellow).

Sound spectrographs of the phrases in each theme follow.

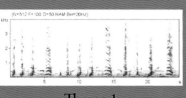

Theme 1

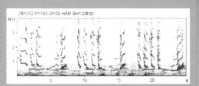

Theme 2

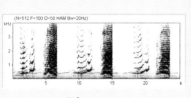

Theme 3

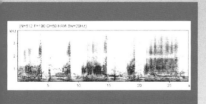

Theme 4

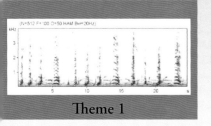

Theme 1

Unique Characteristics

The humpback song is unique in that it gradually changes in composition as it is being sung. That is, small changes in song units will change phrase composition and, in turn, entire themes. (For example, *aaab aaab* in Theme 1 may change to *ab ab*, then eventually drop out altogether.) Yet all the singers in a population sing the same version of the ever-changing song at any one time. Researchers do not know how this is achieved.

Varying Rates of Change

The rate of song change varies — the reason is unknown. Humpback songs studied in Bermuda and Hawaii in the 1970s and 80s changed gradually, with the entire song composition turning over in four or five years. A more recent study in the late 90s off the east coast of Australia showed potential for more rapid change, with the whales there adopting a song from a western Australia population in its entirety over just a two-year period.

To listen to these themes go to
www.whaletrust.org

A particularly cooperative whale appears to sing into the hydrophone. He alternated between singing and investigating the boat.

The challenge for researchers is to take the characteristics of the song and add them to our developing picture of singer behavior (that is, the context of singing) and develop a hypothesis on song function.

In summary, the clues to song function are:

- Singing occurs in and around the breeding season.

- Only males are singers.

- Singers sing until joined by other males for brief (usually), non-agonistic interactions then split up, although at times they form pairs or trios.

- Singing and joining are interchangeable behavior patterns, with a single male filling both roles over a period of hours.

- Males may sing when accompanying females, which leads to other males joining (similar to when a female is not present).

- There has been no reliable observation of a female joining a singer (although more subtle interactions not yet documented may be occurring).

- The song is a complex sequence of sounds that progressively changes. Yet all the singers in a population sing essentially the same version at any one time.

Why Do They Sing?

The function of the song has attracted much speculation, but no definitive answer is yet in sight. It has been proposed as a sexual display (to attract mates or signal status to other males), a means of orientation (such as a male spacing mechanism on the breeding grounds or a migratory beacon), a physiological mechanism (to synchronize estrus in females), and even as a type of sonar to locate females. Only a few of these ideas have been investigated beyond the original proposal. Those hypotheses that have received the most attention are discussed below.

Hypothesis 1. **Song is a display by males to attract females and repel males.**

This proposal suggests that the song provides an indication of fitness of the singer and therefore attracts females (as in a lek-type mating system, where males gather to display and females choose among them). In this scenario the song would also be a male spacing mechanism — keeping males separate from each other. There are three major problems with this hypothesis: (1) no evidence that females are attracted to and join singers; (2) males regularly join singers (with brief non-agonistic interactions); and (3) individual differences in song that would likely be the basis for female choice have not been discerned (that is, the songs of all males appear to be the same).

Hypothesis 2. **Song is a display between males to signal status.**

This proposal suggests that the song is part of a dominance-based mating system. The males sort themselves into a hierarchy through displays and fights, and the most dominant animals mate with the most females. In this scenario, the song functions as a display of individual status (thereby maintaining the social order). Research has shown that singing leads to a range of male/male interactions (as would be predicted from this hypothesis). However, in common with a problem facing Hypothesis 1, the differences in song necessary to signal differing male status have not been found. In fact, the opposite is true, as song similarity is a key characteristic. In addition, the rapid

A singer in a classic singing posture just beneath the surface: motionless with nose down and tail up.

changes in song composition are not consistent with the notion of typical mammalian displays of individual status (e.g. antlers).

MEAGAN JONES

Hypothesis 3. **Song is a measure of association between males.**

This proposal suggests that the changing nature of the song (with all singers in a region singing the same version at any one time) provides a measure of geographic association between males and a means of organizing male relationships in the breeding season. In turn, this may govern male cooperative or competitive interactions when around females. This hypothesis does, at least, account for both song characteristics and known singer behavior. It arose when it became apparent that the existing hypotheses above did not account for all the observations. However, it must be tested to determine its validity.

Pulses of Whale Action

There is a flow to behavior in Hawaii. Anyone watching from a boat or shore will notice periods of little surface activity interspersed with bursts of whale action.

The quiet times reflect calmer behavior involving a lone male, two males, or a male/female pair. Surface activity increases when an additional male joins a male escorting a female. The escort defends its position and attempts to chase the challenger away. This often attracts yet more males, leading to one female with multiple, competitive males racing around for hours and miles.

Eventually, the group dissolves, with the peripheral males transitioning into lone behavior such as singing or traveling, and the female with one male escort returning to a resting mode.

Commonly, males sing until joined by another (non-singing) adult male. These interactions are usually brief (minutes) and sociable, involving a few underwater criss-crosses, as shown above, and close parallel surfacings. Then the two generally part, heading in different directions.

Males Joining Singers

The most common interaction of singers, by far, is when a lone (non-singing) adult male joins them. Singing usually (but not always) stops with the joining. The interactions between singer and joiner vary from just a close approach and departure (or drive-by), with the two never surfacing together, to a brief simultaneous surfacing within a whale's length of each other before separation, to longer interactions that include tail lobs, tail throws, breaches, and flippering by one or both whales *(see Actions and Postures, page 210).*

Most of these singer-joiner inter-actions last less than ten minutes and many, just two or three minutes. In some (approximately one in five), the males do not split up immediately, leading to formation of a pair or, with subsequent joining of other males, a larger group. This variability in inter-actions of singers and joiners suggests a range of social relationships between the males (which the song apparently mediates).

Recent research has shown that singer-joiner interactions such as these are often just one of a chain across the breeding grounds. That is, once the two males (singer and joiner) have split up, one or both swim directly to other nearby singers, join and split, then move on to the next singer, and so on. This be-havior certainly serves to connect males throughout the area, but its specific function (in terms of mating strategy) remains unknown.

JIM DARLNG

Joiners

The blows of a single whale are usually sighted several hundred yards from a singer.

The potential joiner may stay at a distance for several surfacings, its dive-times roughly coinciding with the singer's. Some joiners seem to skulk in towards the singer, with two or three blows, a dive below the surface, and so on. Sometimes they decide not to join, with the next blows farther and farther away.

At times there is no hint of a joiner until a 30-ton torpedo zooms in on the singer. At other times one sees nothing, but the song stops and a few seconds later the ex-singer and ex-joiner are sighted moving away in opposite directions. An interaction occurs without researchers being aware of it!

Over a four-hour period and a distance of 13 km, the singer was joined, stopped singing, then itself joined and split from two other singers, then it began singing again.

Darling et al.
2006

Males Around Females

So far, all the behavior described in this chapter has been between males. Now, as females are added to the picture, it becomes a little more complicated. Reciprocal behavior patterns emerge that can be viewed from both male and female perspectives. The description of these patterns will be repeated to some degree in the following chapter from the female point of view.

Accompanying a Female

A common adult male behavior pattern on the breeding grounds is to pair with a female. This male role is most obvious when the female

It should be obvious who the male escort is in this threesome. Escorts can be downright ornery, expending a lot of energy on bluster and intimidation. At times it is not clear what is aimed at the female and what is aimed at intruders.

has a calf, thereby forming the easily recognizable mother, calf, and escort group. However, a male may also escort a female that does not have a calf, and all that is apparent to the casual observer is a pair of adults. Due to the different stages in the female reproductive cycle (with and without a calf), one might expect a corresponding difference in the male companion behavior or role. But, if it exists, it has yet to be discerned.

86% of mothers with a calf encountered were accompanied by an escort.

Glockner-Ferrari and Ferrari
1985

The escort, stationed below a resting female, will defend his position against male intruders.

It may be that the escort affiliates with a mother long enough to (i) detect if ovulating postpartum and if so remain, (ii) detect if non-ovulating and if so move on, or (iii) detect if mated, and perhaps an additional attempt made. Escort presence could also involve post-copulatory "guarding" behavior.

Mobley and Herman 1985

The behavior of both male/female and male/female/calf groups when not interacting with, or avoiding, other males is often calm, with the animals stationary and resting. In these situations, the adults typically dive for 10–20 minutes, surface for three or four breaths, and then dive again. Some years ago researchers began to call such male/female pairs without a calf "breath-holders," indicating that from the researchers' point of view this is about all they did (this term has stuck). The only obvious difference between these two male/female group types is the calf.

The escort male generally shadows the female. If she is settled and resting, so is the escort. If she is traveling, the escort is usually within a whale's length of her. The escort's breathing and dive patterns generally follow those of the female. In a typical resting situation where the female is motionless, the escort will position himself just off to one side or below, also motionless. Escorts occasionally sing, but most often are quiet. A singing escort may interrupt his normal singing-breathing rhythm in order to follow the female, emphasizing his awareness of her location and behavior.

These male/female pairs are commonly joined by other male(s), upon which the escort usually (but not always) becomes markedly agitated. This involves a range of aggressive behavior from the escort, such as charging the intruder with bubbles streaming from its blowhole, in apparent attempts (some successful, some not) to chase the joining male away. Generally the female (and calf if present) moves away during this male/male interaction. The two males keep pace with the female and often other males in the vicinity rush in to join, thus forming the typical surface active or competitive group described in the next section. The escort (often termed the principal escort when several males are present) may be displaced by another male, or may manage to maintain his position.

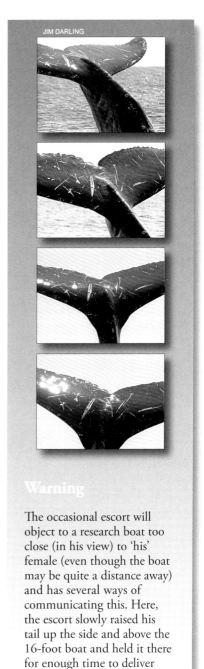

JIM DARLING

Warning

The occasional escort will object to a research boat too close (in his view) to 'his' female (even though the boat may be quite a distance away) and has several ways of communicating this. Here, the escort slowly raised his tail up the side and above the 16-foot boat and held it there for enough time to deliver the message.

What, Then, Is the Role of the Escort?

It is clear the escort defends, with substantial aggressiveness, his role of accompanying a female. (In fact, some of these escorts don't really differentiate between challenging whales, small research boats, or underwater observers!) However, his reasons for escorting are not entirely understood.

Actually, some of the very first reports in the 1970s assumed the escort was a female and played an allomaternal (assistant mother) role in protecting the calf. At first glance, this seemed to make sense. Even after the determination that escorts were males, there was speculation that they played a protective role towards mother and calf. This was partially due to a 1950s description of a humpback whale escort 'defending' a mother and calf in conflict with killer whales. That is, some observers interpreted the typical wariness of escorts to intruders, both whale and human alike, as protective of the mother and calf.

However, other researchers suggested the escort is primarily interested in mating rather than protecting the female (and calf). One report noted a mother that had a calf in four consecutive years was accompanied by an escort on each of seven sightings during that period. Another report suggested the duration of the escort/female affiliation may extend beyond courtship and mating if the male engages in post-mating 'guarding' behavior against other males.

The explanation of the escort may be a mixture of the above. The female tolerates the male since it may provide protection against harassment from other males, with the pay-off from the male's view that he will be nearest when she comes into estrus and is receptive to mating.

Competition for Access to Females

Surface active or competitive groups are the most striking humpback behavior on the breeding grounds, characterized by fast-traveling whales and high-energy activity. They can often be seen from miles away as three, four, ten or more blows shoot up in quick succession as the action moves across the horizon at high speed. These groups are composed of multiple males competing for access to a female, presumably in estrus. It is not known if mating occurs during this action, but it seems a possibility as extended penes and close rolling and

When several males follow a female the action is complex. There is competition, with the escort (or principal escort) nearest the female fiercely taking on all challengers, and at the same time there may be cooperation between pairs or even trios of males to outmaneuver him.

contact have been observed. On the other hand, the movement is often so rapid, some doubt mating could occur.

Competitive groups are typically composed of one female with or without a calf (termed the nuclear animal by some authors), usually in the lead, but at times in the center, of multiple males. (There are several reported cases of two females present with multiple males, but these are exceptional.)

This group moves rapidly about the area 'picking up' additional males and 'losing' other males in the process. The principal escort (nearest the female) is invariably the most agitated and active, clearly defending his position with exuberant lunges and bubblestreams, high-speed chases, and blocks of incoming whales. These groups are characterized by bursts of speed (10 knots and more) and changes in direction as the secondary escorts (or challengers) apparently attempt to outmaneuver the

This competition (amongst males) involves fluke thrashes, the blowing of bubblestreams and physical contact, some of which appears designed to hurt an opponent — bleeding wounds are seen on the competing escorts.

Tyack and Whitehead
1983

Male humpback whales threaten and fight with each other, mostly over access to a female. This behavior ranges from threat displays to fierce physical contact.

Threats include bubblestreaming, underwater blows, a posture with back arched and head above the surface (head lift), gulping air at the surface (resulting in impressively extended throat pleats) and then explosively releasing the air underwater, lunging and/or slapping the chin on the surface, clapping the jaws open and shut, and directing a tail lash at another animal without hitting it *(see Actions and Postures)*.

These displays can shift into physical contact involving blocking and chasing, which may include tail lashes (even slapping another male's head with the flukes), rear body throws, and collisions. The whale's weapons are its tail, whole body and, at times, its head. The combatants may receive minor wounds such as bloody head knobs, dorsal fins, and tail stocks. Many of the scars and scratches that decorate some whales, particularly males, result from these encounters.

JIM DARLING

JIM DARLING

FLIP NICKLIN © National Geographic Society reprinted with permission

principal escort. Most of the interaction occurs between the principal escort and one or two of the challengers, with other animals following along on the periphery. Occasionally the secondary escorts replace the principal escort, but most often they just leave the group after a period ranging from minutes to many hours.

Social Sounds

The whales in competitive groups may make a wide range of loud, energetic, underwater sounds ranging from whistles and screeches to grunts and growls, collectively referred to as "social sounds." These sounds are a 'force' on the breeding grounds as, on hearing them, males will frequently interrupt other activity, such as singing, and rapidly travel for miles to join the group.

To date there is only one study that has specifically investigated social sounds. This work involved spending months in Hawaii maneuvering well in front of competitive groups and recording them as they passed by, then correlating sounds with observations of the groups themselves.

The study found social sounds:

- Occurred almost exclusively in groups containing three or more whales and were rarely heard near single whales, pairs, or mother/calf groups.

- Increased dramatically in number when a new whale entered a group.

- Increased in number with group size, suggesting that each group member contributed to overall sound production.

- Could be overlapping, that is, from two or more whales vocalizing simultaneously. (This led to speculation that competing males produce the sounds, possibly as threat gestures.)

- Could be rare in some large groups that showed little surface activity.

During these multiple male/single female competitive interactions, a wide range of loud sounds — including groans, hiccups, whistles, screams, and thrums — are emitted by the males.

This researcher speculated that social sounds act to demonstrate aggression or agitation as adult males compete for temporary social dominance within the group and thereby closeness to the female.

Humpbacks appear to sense and respond to large groups of whales up to at least nine km (over five miles) away. Acoustic cues are likely candidates.

Tyack and Whitehead 1983

101

Five males are following a mother, calf, and escort. The question of how the five relate to each other is open — that is, do some or all coordinate in some way to try to dislodge the escort?

Observations of pairs of males acting as a non-competitive unit against other males, or attempting to corral a female by one chasing and the other blocking, suggest some level of cooperation.

Cooperation for Access to a Female

In contrast to male competition on the breeding grounds, there are suggestions of cooperative behavior among some males to gain access to a female. This may include the formation of male coalitions that work together and against other males in competitive situations, or possibly in attempts to constrain the movements of a female.

The idea of male pairs or coalitions working together or cooperating against other males in competitive groups first arose from observations on the West Indies humpback whale breeding grounds. As early as the 1980s, when male competitive behavior was first being described, one researcher noted male pairs working as cooperative units within competitive groups.

Similar observations from this and other breeding areas have appeared sporadically in the literature ever since. For example, in the mid-1990s,

Australian researchers noted a male pair that moved between competitive groups and engaged in agonistic displays with other animals, but not with each other. They speculated that, if subordinate animals join competitive groups together rather than alone, the odds of one of them outmaneuvering the dominant males, and subsequently mating, may increase.

There are also a few observations of a team of two males seemingly cooperating to corral a female. The most complete of these to date, from Hawaii, involved a singer and joiner that formed a pair and immediately approached a nearby mother with calf. The ex-singer, bubblestreaming, chased the female, while the ex-joiner appeared to block by repeatedly crossing directly in front of her.

This possible connection between singing, joining, and male cooperation raises interesting questions about the function of the song. A further hint at this potential link is an observation of a singer being joined, then another male joining this pair to form a trio that immediately swam together to a passing competitive group. However, clear observations connecting singers and joiners with cooperative behavior around a female are few and far between. Therefore, the questions of if, and how, these behavior patterns may be connected, although very intriguing, are far from answered.

The possibility that males form coalitions cannot be dismissed. That is, humpback males may cooperate in their effort to secure access to a female.

Clapham et al. 1992

Most male/male associations were characterized by non-agonistic and occasionally cooperative interactions.

Brown and Corkeron 1995

The pair (singer and joiner) were joined by a third male and the trio rushed to a passing competitive group as a unit.

Darling and Bérubé 2001

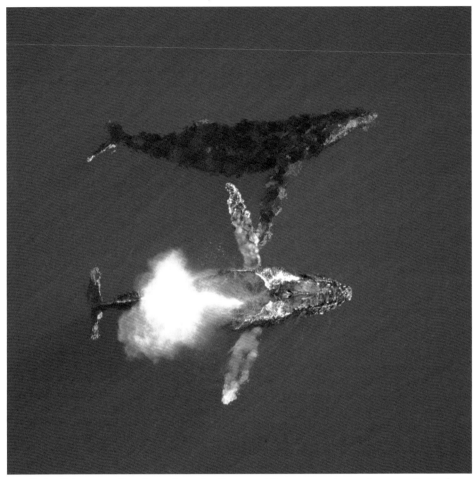

Potential cooperation in mating situations and the apparent care (or guarding) of an associate that died in a competitive group hint that humpback males may have more complex relationships than initially considered.

Males Caring for Other Males?

One of the more unusual observations of humpback male behavior occurred on February 9, 1996 in waters off Lahaina, Maui. A whale-watching boat reported a whale had died in a competitive group, and researchers rushed to the scene. (This is the only documented case of a humpback whale dying in the midst of a competitive group.) The dead whale was a male. Another adult male remained beside the dead whale for over four hours, alternating between clasping it with its flippers or stationing itself beside or below, and on several occasions placed himself between the dead whale and a diver filming, directing tail lashes and other threat gestures at the diver.

One of several possible explanations of this behavior was that it was a form of helping (epimeletic) behavior between males. There are reports from whaling ships of adult humpbacks standing by or supporting those injured or killed by harpoons. If this was the explanation for the behavior, it seems more reflective of extended associations and cooperation between some individual males rather than universal competition, as has often been presumed.

The interpretation of the behaviors of the live whales toward the dead whale remains problematic but may offer a new perspective on social relations among male humpbacks on the winter grounds.

Pack et al.
1998

Mature males travel to the breeding grounds to mate with as many females as possible. All male behavior — the singing, joining singers, escorting a female, and competing, individually or in cooperative coalitions — is related to this one objective. Researchers have described many male behavior patterns relatively well (compared to female patterns) over the last thirty years. However, we do not yet understand how all these patterns are 'connected' to each other or, for many, what their specific function is within the mating system.

Mating — The Male Perspective

Quick Info

What do males do in Hawaii?

Adult male humpback whales look for receptive females, pair with them, and attempt to defend that position against challengers, or they challenge existing escorts for access to a female.

What is humpback whale song, who sings, why?

Humpback whale song is a complex series of sounds, typically ten to fifteen minutes long, repeated over and over by adult males during the breeding season. The song gradually changes as it is being sung, yet all singers sing essentially the same version at any one time. The function of the song is not known.

What follows singing?

Singers most often sing until joined by non-singing adult males. The interaction typically lasts just a few minutes and is rarely aggressive, then the pair usually splits and heads in different directions.

What is an escort?

Escort is the term given an adult male that accompanies a female. It is most often used in cases where the female has a calf, but similar behavior occurs when the female is without a calf. The escort defends his position with the female from other males.

What is a surface active group?

A surface active or competitive group (interchangeable terms) is composed of a single female, presumably in or near estrus, and multiple males competing for access to her. A principal escort, nearest the female, is most active in defending his position against the challengers.

Do males fight with each other?

Yes, males fight. These events range from threats where there is no physical clash to all-out collisions and blows. Males fight when competing with each other around a female in estrus.

What are social sounds?

Social sounds are a wide variety of sounds including whistles, screeches, grunts, and growls made by males in competitive groups. They might be threats.

Do males cooperate with each other?

At times, males apparently cooperate to corral (or otherwise gain access to) a female in estrus. They may form cooperative pairs that work together and against other males in competitive situations.

Chapter 5

Mating — The Female Perspective

By traveling to Hawaii, female humpback whales make themselves accessible to sexually active males — a bunch of them. If mating is not an objective, they are definitely in the wrong place. But what happens between a female and the males? What forces are at work? The interactions that occur between her arrival and departure a few weeks later, newly pregnant, are unexplored (scientific) territory.

If a humpback male's biggest challenge in mating is simply finding a female in estrus, a female's may be to mate successfully with a high-quality (fit, healthy) male with the least possible energy expenditure. In other words, the female may want to be picky, but not so picky the energetic cost is higher than the value of the male upgrade. The intriguing question for researchers is, how does she achieve this? Does she simply swim onto the breeding grounds and make herself available? Does she behave in a way that encourages male competition? Does she more actively choose males with specific attributes?

Knowledge of female humpback behavior in a mating context may be the least-known aspect of this species' behavior. This chapter explores what we do know regarding the female perspective, describes some possible but unproven scenarios, and shows that researchers have more questions than answers.

Pairing With, Avoiding, And (Perhaps) Choosing Males

The female whale in Hawaii is almost always (either by choice or coercion) accompanied by one or more males. She may be calmly accompanied by a single adult male or pursued by several competitive males. In the latter case, she is eventually left with one male companion, which may or may not be her original escort. There is little doubt that a female does not always seek this male attention and at times tries to discourage or escape it. (This may be the reason for cooperative male behavior, as it is much harder to escape two males than one.) The ultimate question here is whether a female chooses, either passively or actively, specific males over others.

When on the breeding grounds and therefore fasting, females may behave: (1) to accomplish mating while spending the least amount of time (for overall energetic considerations); (2) to maximize the number of males and minimize the number of females encountered.

Gabriele
1992

Female behavior is as subtle as male behavior is overt. They often seem to be doing very little, lying absolutely still in the water — but in any larger view, they are probably orchestrating much of the male behavior around them.

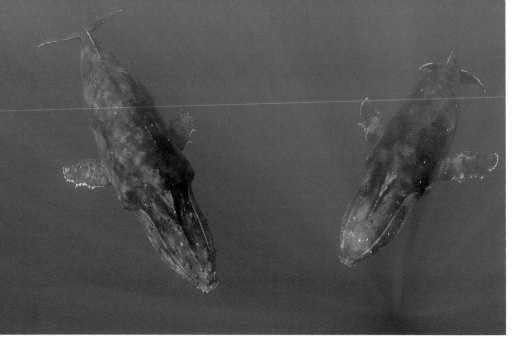

A portion of the female humpback whales that migrate to Hawaii are present only to mate — having recently weaned a yearling or completed a non-reproductive year. (That is, they are not in late pregnancy or with newborn.) They are often found paired with a male.

Female Roles

Overall, female behavior patterns in Hawaii fall into two realms: mating and then birth and newborn care. Intuitively, these should be quite separate, even mutually exclusive, but it's not entirely clear that this is the case.

Mature females that come to Hawaii are either:

- Not pregnant, having just completed a year of child-care and recently weaned a yearling (which may still be present or nearby), or having completed a non-reproductive year.

- In late pregnancy and about to give birth (or with a brand-new calf presumably born en route).

For the first category of females, the objective is to mate, then return to the feeding grounds. For the second category, while the primary objective is presumably birth, protection of the newborn, and preparation of the calf for return to the feeding grounds *(see Chapter 3)*, these new mothers undergo estrus and are also involved in mating activity.

Successful mating may involve maximizing contact with males, as this would seem the best way to accomplish the objective. In contrast, successful birth and newborn care may involve minimizing contact with rowdy males to conserve energy and protect the calf. This seems to make sense. However, we find all females, whether or not they have a newborn tagging along, involved in similar (presumably mating-related) behavior.

There are several possible explanations for this conduct. (1) Perhaps the energetic mating activity does not impact the newborn and it is not critical for new mothers to minimize contact with males and/or the value of the potential pregnancy is great enough to risk the newborn. (2) Male interaction with mothers is solely harassment and coercion, near impossible to avoid, and not a female reproductive strategy. (3) There are in fact differences in how single females, and mothers with a calf, interact with males, but they have not yet been discerned.

These questions aside, following is a very basic approach to female humpback behavior in Hawaii: what we see females do, and what we don't see females do.

Many female humpbacks arrive in Hawaii in late pregnancy and are present to give birth and/or to nurture newborn. However, with calf alongside, they may also be involved in mating activity, often escorted by one or more males.

What We See

On any day of the winter, where are the females and what are they doing? The answer to these questions changes somewhat over the season. To start, the proportion of females without a calf versus females with a calf reverses itself as the season progresses. That is, from December to February, a female is more likely to be seen without a calf, but from February through April is far more likely to be found with a calf. However, apart from newborn care, female behavior appears similar whether she is a current mother or not.

The three social situations in which a female (with and without a calf) is encountered are:

Female with an Adult Male

A female is often found paired with an adult male. In the second half of the season, as mentioned above, most females in an adult pair also have a calf in tow.

The female in these social units is often stationary, apparently resting. This suggests she accepts or at least tolerates the male companion. However, on occasion the female is obviously fleeing, suggesting that the presence of males (or at least some males) is not always acceptable.

Female with Multiple Males

Throughout the winter season, females are found in front of, or otherwise the focus of, multiple males in competitive groups. The females are either being chased by, or are leading, the competitive males. Competitive groups occur around females without a calf and females with a calf, probably indicating she is in or near estrus in both cases.

Female Discouraging Males

Female humpbacks at times behave in ways that make it quite clear they would prefer that the attentive males get lost. In scientific terms, the females appear to influence selection of mates in several overt ways. Our understanding of this behavior is thin, but there is little doubt it occurs.

At times, females accept the presence of males; at other times (*as shown above*), the female flees, clearly trying to lose the unwanted company.

For example, it is apparent a female may avoid unwanted mating by raising her fluke, tail stock, and genital region vertically above the surface of the water and out of reach of males. The problem with this maneuver (for the female) is it means her head is underwater and eventually she has to breathe. There are also observations of females behaving aggressively towards sub-adult males, a social group that may be pests at mating time. Other examples of females discouraging or avoiding males include leading males into shallows, or to boats, where they seem to 'rub them off' and lose them.

Current descriptions of this behavior are based on just a few observations and it clearly deserves further study. What is not known is whether this 'discouragement' occurs only when the female is avoiding all males or just certain males. The latter possibility may be evidence of deliberate female choice of mates. In other words, these observations could be just the tip of the iceberg of female mating strategy.

On seven occasions (in Hawaii) a female led males repeatedly towards vessels, or the shoreline, resulting in either the replacement of an escort, or the retreat of the pursuing males.

Glockner-Ferrari and Ferrari 1985

A nuclear animal (that is, a female) that does not wish to be courted may lead the surface active group into areas where coral heads are abundant (on Silver Bank in the Caribbean) in an effort to shake off aggressive males.

Mattila et al. 1989

This photograph shows a mature female humpback not accompanied by any males. This is a fairly uncommon occurrence on the breeding grounds, even for mothers with newborn calves.

What We Don't (Or Rarely) See

Females Are Rarely Alone

An adult female is not often found alone on the breeding grounds. This claim comes from studies that analyzed multiple sightings of known (photo-identified) individual females and the social situation they were seen in on each sighting — females were almost always accompanied by males.

Another way of approaching this subject is to look at females whose sex is, in fact, determined at a glance — those with a calf. The proportion of mothers with an escort is consistently (from several studies) around 85 percent, meaning only three out of twenty are without a male companion. If this ratio can be applied to females without a calf (and it is not at all clear it can be, as one expects current mothers may not encourage males as much as potential mothers), it means some females are finding time alone without males or babies. But remember, females whose priority is pregnancy are not being successful if they are alone.

Females Do Not Associate with Other Females

Female/female interactions and associations on the breeding grounds are very rare (in complete contrast to male/male ones). The handful of observations (in over thirty years) of two females in the same group suggests it is accidental (such as when two competitive groups run into each other by chance) and remedied quickly. In fact, mothers with a calf often actively avoid each other, altering course to increase the distance from other such pairs. Curiously, in other baleen species such as gray whales, the females do not seem to avoid each other. Moreover, on the feeding grounds, humpback females associate freely in groups.

Females Do Not Join Singers

Females are not seen approaching or joining male singers, although males escorting a female sometimes sing. In one study in Hawaii, the sex of whales that joined singers was determined genetically (through collection of skin biopsies), and none was a female. This finding has been supported with similar studies on other humpback whale breeding grounds.

In 27 repeat sightings of females without a calf, all were accompanied by males on each sighting. Mothers with calves were accompanied by a male in 102 of 123 observations (83%).

Darling
1983

JIM DARLING

Copulation?

Copulation has not been observed — therefore, it is only a presumption that females identified in pairs and multiple male groups are involved in mating behavior.

The following observations within pairs or larger groups of adults suggest mating or attempted mating:

- Females followed or chased by males.
- 'Nosing' of genital area by males, possibly checking for estrus.
- Excited rolling and flippering in close proximity or contact with other whales.
- Female tail arching, or contorting of the tail stock into an "S" shape, suggesting presentation of the genital area.
- Female rolling, or extending tail out of the water, to put her genital area above the surface, suggesting avoidance.
- Extended penes.

119

Mating Situations

When does mating occur and in what groups? One approach to this question is to take sightings of females with tiny babies and rewind history 11–12 months, which should lead us to the time of mating situations. Multi-year studies based on the identification of individual animals allow us to do this. All the repeat sightings of an individual female (sex determined by presence of a calf in one of the sightings) over a series of years are analyzed, and in some cases a female that gave birth one year had also been seen the previous year involved in other behavior. So we connect the two. There is no guarantee that this exercise establishes when mating occurs, but at this point it is all we have to work with.

Pairs of adult whales, surfacing and diving together, are a common sight in the early winter season in Hawaii. One is a female, the other a male.

Collective research efforts have provided a number of examples of females observed with single males or in multiple male groups during one winter, then re-identified with a calf the following winter. This is also true of females that gave birth in successive years. These observations, combined with the understood gestation period of 11–12 months, indicate the possibility that mating occurred in the pair or multiple-male group. Specific examples are provided in the following plate.

In the previous chapter we described the two social situations or groups that include both males and a female from the former's perspective. We review them here, but from the female viewpoint.

Rewinding History: When Does Mating Occur?

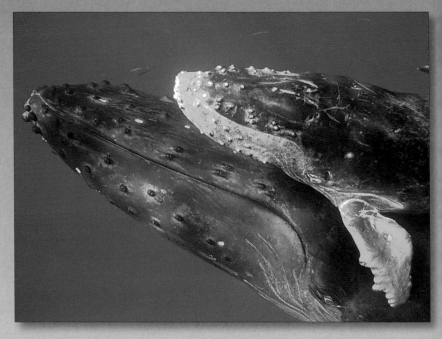

One way of estimating when and where mating occurs is to look at what a female was doing 11 to 12 months (gestation period) prior to being sighted with a new calf. Long-term photo-identification studies allow this re-winding of history. Specific examples follow.

Female in a Pair

Example 1 A female (#13) identified as one of a pair (Mar. 3, 1980) had a calf the following season. The other member of the pair on this date was not sexed, but had been seen in a group of 5–7 adults earlier in the day, suggesting it was a male. This pair was milling, with significant surface activity including flippering, breaching, rolling belly up, and one animal swimming upside down close to the surface just prior to blowing.

Example 2 A female (#17) was identified twice in a pair with different partners (Jan. 30 and Feb. 18, 1980) a year before she was seen with a calf. On January 30 her partner was a known male. The only behavior noted was that the male lifted his head above the water when he was swimming beside the female. He had a raw, bloody area on his peduncle, probably the result of fighting with other males over access to the female.

Female in a Larger Group (of males)

Example 1 This female (#15) had been identified in a group of four or more adults a year (Feb. 18, 1980) before she was identified with a calf (Feb. 15, 1981). The behavior of this larger group included flippering and rolling, along with a variety of apparently aggressive interactions including head lifts, chin slaps, jaw claps, tail lashes, and bubblestreams. Specific behavior patterns were not correlated with individuals.

Example 2 A female (#18) was identified in large groups (Feb. 1 and 6, 1980) a year before she was found with a calf. On February 1 she was seen with a group of four or more adults and later in a group of eight or more adults. The behavior patterns noted were flippering, head lifts, jaw claps, tail lobs, and underwater blows. This example also indicates that a female may be close enough to estrus over a period of six days to attract males.

It is important to emphasize that the inferences made here are just that — they are the best guesses with the information we have. The unanswered questions of when, where, and with whom successful mating occurs are a source of continued frustration to researchers. Clearly, the answers are fundamental to understanding behavior on the breeding grounds, but to date they have been elusive.

Female/male pairs often
appear synchronized in their
underwater movements.

Female/Male Pair

Female/male pairs are relatively stable (in comparison to larger groups or male pairs), often maintaining a calm, exclusive union for hours to a day or longer. Instances of conclusive sexing of both individuals (when a calf is not present) combined with extended behavioral observations are limited, although studies addressing this are underway. General patterns that are likely female/male follow below.

Often the female/male pair is stationary, except when surfacing. They make near-synchronized long dives of 20–30 minutes or more. Underwater observations indicate these pairs dive to approximately 50–100 feet (15–30 m) and stop. (As mentioned before, these long dives have caused this behavior to be dubbed "breath-holding.")

Typically one whale is in a horizontal position, and the other in a more vertical, head-down position. Beyond this, there is little obvious interaction or activity between the whales (this calmness is at times interrupted with brief bouts of rolling, flippering, or breaching by one or both animals). Occasionally, the male has been observed singing, although this is an exception rather than the rule.

The development or instigation of these pairs is not understood, but outwardly they are (at least temporarily) mutually acceptable as there is no obvious escape behavior by the female.

Eight females were seen as one of a pair of adults or in large groups of adults in the years they were not identified with a calf. Two mothers that gave birth in consecutive years were accompanied by either a single escort or multiple males in the year before the consecutive birth.

Darling
1983

In 13 of 16 cases where females with a calf had also been seen the previous season, they were in a pair.

Gabriele
1992

The most likely explanations are that a female is approaching estrus and accepting of the male attention, or alternatively, having mated, she is allowing a guard against unwanted attention.

As discussed earlier *(see Chapter 4)*, these pairs tend to persist until another adult (male) joins, potentially leading to the formation of a larger competitive group. The pair may re-form after the larger group breaks up.

Females Leading Multiple Males

Adult females with or without a calf can be followed by groups of males (anywhere from two to twenty), with all the attendant aggressive activity described in the previous chapter. The big question here is, are these females victims of male harassment and coercion, or are they the instigators and beneficiaries of the male competition? We don't know and, of course, it could be either in different situations.

JIM DARLING

One scenario is that the competitive groups are ultimately a test of male fitness, with the most 'fit' (strongest, smartest) gaining access to the female. In this case, the female, by moving rapidly in front of the group and leading it over substantial distances, both avoids unwanted mating and attracts as many males as possible, thereby increasing the level of competition in the group and ultimately gaining a preferable mate.

The other possibility is that the female does not want to be hounded by a bunch of males. It has been speculated that a female may tolerate a single male escort solely because he may discourage the attention of other males and reduce this harassment. This seems to make sense for mothers with a small calf, where the energy expenditure used in fleeing from males could be an impediment to the calf's survival.

Mating may occur in the midst of surface active groups, but it has not been documented. Commotion on the surface like this is often seen, but it's usually not clear if the female is in the middle somewhere or if it's all competing males.

Do Females Choose Their Mates Based On Their Song?

The idea that females may select mates based on listening to their songs is undoubtedly the best-known unproven hypothesis regarding the breeding behavior of humpbacks. This view has received a great deal of attention in twenty-five or so years of scientific and popular publications, yet there exists no evidence for it. There are very few actual observations of females joining singers, song playback experiments have failed to attract females, and there are strong indications that the song is primarily a signal between males.

Advocates of the "female choice of mate by song" view, in acknowledgment of the lack of observations of females actually joining singers, have proposed an alternative scenario still based on female choice. They speculate that a female need not approach a singer, but instead provide an 'invitation' for the male to approach her. This idea suggests a female may indicate her preference for a particular singer and hence song by whether she allows the pursuing singer to join her, or perhaps with a return vocalization (that has not been heard nor listened for). In this view, the song may not serve to bring females directly to the singer, but may still serve as a basis for female selection.

Another suggestion is that the song may simply allow a female to locate and evaluate singers, and she may lead a competitive group towards the loudest, deepest song she hears, inviting the singer to compete. It is important to note that these possibilities have not been investigated, or even observed.

We are just beginning to understand the mating behavior of female humpback whales. In contrast to the overt singing and fighting of males, female behavior is often subtle — so much so that it tempts the impression they are doing very little. In fact, though, it is probable the females are instigating and even 'managing' much of the behavior we see. There is much yet to be revealed and there are compelling questions for researchers who wish to explore the behavior of female humpback whales.

Although a common notion, there is no evidence females choose males based on their song.

Mating — The Female Perspective

Quick Info

What do female humpbacks do in Hawaii?

Females come to Hawaii to either mate or to give birth. Some do both in the same season. Estrus females need to associate with males, whereas birthing females do not (and their behavior may vary accordingly).

Who are females with?

On the breeding grounds, we see females accompanied by a single male (that is, in a pair) and in larger surface active groups where she is chased by (or leads) multiple males. Adult females are rarely alone on the breeding grounds.

Do females associate with each other?

Female humpback whales do not purposely associate with, and seem to actively avoid, each other on the breeding grounds. Groups with more than one female have been observed, but these are short-lived and appear to occur by chance.

When does mating occur?

Mating has not been documented. However, there are examples of individual females identified on the breeding grounds about a year before being seen with a calf. At that time they were either one of a pair or the focus of a competitive group. The odds are mating occurs in these situations.

What is the female mating strategy?

We do not know. The question is whether or not females simply move onto the breeding grounds and let the males compete — with, in theory, the strongest or fittest male winning access — or whether they select mates in a more specific way.

Do females choose their mate by listening to his song?

There is no evidence that this occurs, but the idea persists.

Chapter 6

Newborns and Juveniles

Through the eventual synchrony of a female's receptivity and a male's persistence, a pregnancy results. The mother-to-be then heads for summer feeding grounds to fuel for a successful gestation and healthy baby. The following winter, near term (or as a new mother), she again passes through the channels of the Hawaiian Islands. This chapter picks up the story here.

Birth is not easily (actually, so far never) documented. Our earliest glimpse of a newborn humpback is generally when a tiny light-colored, wrinkled, bent-dorsal-finned creature puffs alongside its relatively massive mother. The nearshore habitat new mothers seek out makes them the closest whales to human activity. Calves spend their first weeks traveling, resting, nursing, and playing. Then they accompany their mothers across the North Pacific to distant feeding grounds.

A year after birth, the young animals migrate to Hawaii with their mothers. Some break the maternal bond en route, others on the breeding grounds. Consequently, there is a significant youth culture in Hawaiian waters comprising these yearlings and older juveniles that have not yet reached sexual maturity. These young whales are often on the periphery of adult activity, mimicking their behavior and interacting with mature males.

Maternal Priorities

Since the birth of a humpback whale has not been documented, the specific behavior patterns of the mother immediately before, during, and after birth are not known. It is likely the mother's behavior is geared towards rest, nursing, and protection of the young. The last of these endeavors may have three fronts: (1) avoiding, or at least controlling, interactions with sexually active males; (2) avoiding interactions with other mothers with a calf; and (3) guarding against potential predators.

Those Persistent Males

The need for separation of mother and newborn from the male harassment surrounding mating activity (at least at critical times) may be a major driving force of mother/young behavior in Hawaii. A female's options for accomplishing this separation in the short term include simply dodging the activity—for instance, moving to inshore, shallow waters. In the longer term, seasonal adjustment of birth times may have occurred (birth before reaching Hawaii or at least out of sync with peak mating times). Both of these strategies may be beneficial in terms of health of the newborn.

Humpback mothers maneuver through a sea of male attention, not all invited. Consequently, they spend a lot of time very near shore, shifting locations, or in outright flight.

Mothers with newborn calves steer clear of other mothers, moving away to keep their distance.

Avoiding the Neighbors

Mothers with a young calf actively avoid any close association with other mothers with young. This can pose a challenge in peak season when the density of these mother/calf groups can be as high as one every several hundred square yards or so. If a mother and calf are traveling, they must keep changing course; if stationary, they must interrupt rest or nursing and shift locations to avoid interaction.

Several explanations for mother and calf avoidance of other groups have been proposed, including the possibility of such interactions leading to:

- Premature social interactions for the calf
- Increased energy expenditure
- Interruption of nursing bouts
- Mistaken imprinting or nursing attempts
- Separation of calves from mothers
- Injury to calves

However, just to complicate this, remember that females without a calf do not associate either, so perhaps the explanation lies within the broader female reproductive strategy, rather than just how these interactions may impact calves.

The First Weeks

Humpback babies are born into some of the most beautiful water in the world — the warm, glimmering blues of the subtropics. They emerge into an environment saturated with sound, with singing all around them, day and night, through the first weeks of life. They soon learn their boundaries, the surface, the vital interface between water and the air they breathe, which they will try to break through with their antics, and the sea floor when in the shallows with a resting mother.

In their first days, calves experience the warmth and clarity of the sea, the connection to a large community of whales, and no shortage of activity as their mother navigates through encounters with one or many males. They learn about fish that follow them around feeding on bits of skin, dolphins that bow-ride on mom, boats and researchers and, perhaps, predators.

Predators

Little is known about predators on humpback whales in Hawaii. We don't even really know whether predation is a significant problem or whether threats are minimal and this is one reason the mothers-to-be come to Hawaii. There *are* potential predators in Hawaiian waters, including groups of large dolphins called false killer whales *(Pseudorca)*, and pygmy killer whales *(Feresa)* — their names hint at their voraciousness. True killer whales *(Orcinus orca)* are occasionally seen in Hawaiian waters, but are certainly more common (and more of a threat to humpbacks) in cooler seas. Then, of course, there are the ever-present tiger sharks.

Schools of false and pygmy killer whales could be a factor in mother/newborn behavior. Since the 1980s, there have been reports of false killer whales harassing and possibly attacking mothers and newborn calves. One fisherman watched a group of false killer whales attack a calf off the Big Island, leaving substantial blood and a missing calf. It seems that some level of harassment of humpback mothers with a calf by false killer whales is fairly common, but how often this leads to the injury or death of a calf is not known.

Humpback calves, like most young mammals, rely on their mothers for protection.

Tiger sharks are, without any doubt, a major predator in the Hawaiian breeding area, and they are not known for fussiness in what they eat. There have been several observations of them gorging on dead whales, following sick calves, and even attacking living but injured sub-adults. However, whether they actively or successfully pursue healthy calves is not known.

Options for predator avoidance in the ocean are limited. Shallow water is apparently key to one successful strategy. The shallows reduce the number of directions to guard by eliminating attacks from below and above. They may also confound the echolocation and communication abilities of predatory whales. This could be the (or at least one) explanation for mother and newborn preference for inshore habitat.

Maternal females may use shallower water to avoid harassment and injury to calves from sexually active males, turbulent offshore conditions or predators.

Smultea
1994

BILL SCOTT

Safe Haven?

The level of predation on newborn whales in Hawaiian waters may be low compared to other parts of the humpbacks' range.

However, there are potential predators, including schools of large black dolphins called false killer whales that, at times, will harass and apparently kill a calf. In the photos above a humpback mother blocks two false killer whales from her calf.

The actual birth of a humpback whale has yet to be documented, but tiny babies such as this one (only days or even hours old) are often encountered.

A Birth — Who Will See It First?

A most striking non-observation in Hawaii is the birth of a baby humpback whale. With tens of thousands of whale-watch hours each season, as well as the presence of multiple researchers for over thirty years, a birth has not been documented. It's amazing.

To be specific, a birth may well have been seen, and there are one or two reports each winter where the observers have been convinced. However, it is yet to be documented — that is, to date no photographs or scientific observations of the actual delivery exist.

At the same time, there is little question that birth does occur during the winter season in Hawaii. The evidence is this:

- Studies from whaling operations clearly show that term fetuses and birth coincide with winter months.

- In Hawaii, observations of tiny calves with folded dorsal fins and crease marks (clearly within days if not hours of birth) are common.

- A humpback whale placenta (mammalian organ that nourishes the fetus) was found in Hawaii shortly after a very young calf appeared beside an adult.

- One study reported a sighting of a photo-identified female without a calf on January 31 (1981) and with a calf seventeen days later on February 16 (1981), indicating a birth had occurred.

The fact that it is so difficult to see an actual birth may be an indication of just how critical the separation of birth from the ongoing activity (both whale and human) in the region is. Does it occur before the whales reach the Hawaiian Islands? Does it occur at night?

On January 11, 1994, an extremely active adult dove for eight minutes. Upon resurfacing, a very small calf was noted next to the whale. A large placenta was found (in the vicinity) 15 minutes later.

Silvers and Salden 1997

When Do We See Humpback Calves?

The earliest date of a published sighting of a female with a young calf in Hawaii (at the time of writing) is on December 24. However, this is a case where the common knowledge from whale-watching sightings outweighs the published material and certainly young calves have been reported prior to that date.

Early studies (1980s) in Hawaii suggested mothers with newborn calves were relatively rare before the end of January (just two pairs in five seasons in one comprehensive survey). However, there have been no published reports of comparable information in recent years. Anecdotal information suggests calves are more common in the early season today than they were in the 1980s, but this has not been quantified.

These sightings are not birthdays — whereas some of the calves seen in the early winter in Hawaii are tiny (and clearly recent additions), others are a relatively good size and likely weeks to months old. (One more humpback whale enigma: If the larger calves seen in Hawaii are born en route, what is the reason for migrating to Hawaii?)

After the beginning of February, the number of mothers with calves increases markedly (in fact, they are everywhere), and they are among the last groups present at the very end of the season in May and even June.

A bent-over dorsal fin on a tiny, creased calf (*left*) is a sure sign of a very new addition to Hawaii's humpback population.

JIM DARLING

Large Mammal Babies

Newborn humpback whales are like any baby mammal. They are (whale) cute, endearing, and a little out of control. They alternate between bouts of energetic flipping and flopping around the mother, then resting quietly tucked under her flipper or chin, or riding (slipstreaming) above her mouth. They have challenges with coordination and diving. Sometimes they just can't get down to mom resting 20 feet (7 m) below, and end up flopping back to the surface, floating up tail first. Often the calf will twirl its body and swim upside down.

They are very curious. They have no fear of boats or researchers, with mothers often having to retrieve them from these explorations. However, some mothers see no threat in this and appear to continue sleeping as the calf amuses itself with objects in its environment. More than one researcher has been surprised with a calf's nose pressed up against his/her face mask (and wondering just what the mother is thinking at that point!).

Newborns — How Do They Spend Their First Weeks In Hawaii?

In their first few weeks, newborn humpback whales travel (a lot) and then they rest, play and, of course, eat.

Travel — The Most Common Activity!

Mothers with a calf circulate through the main Hawaiian Island chain, as do other humpback whale social groups. Day-to-day resightings of a specific mother and her calf in one location are rare. The purpose, or cause, of this steady movement is not known; perhaps it is part of the swimming regimen preparing the calf for migration, or possibly the result of the mother being pursued or harassed by males.

Travel was by far the most common activity of mothers with calves. . . . Rest was the next most common activity, with the proportion of time spent at rest increasing as calves matured.

Cartwright
2005

The most common mother and calf activity is moving around their winter range. The reasons for this are not clear, but may include getting away from rowdy males or preparing the calf for migration to feeding grounds.

Resting mother, calf, and escort groups are common. The calf cannot hold its breath as long as adults so must rise to the surface by itself every few minutes, then dive again to its mother's side. Above, a calf rises solo to the surface with its mother below, and escort on guard off to one side.

Resting

Mothers with a young calf are often found resting. Typically, the mother lies in a horizontal position at a depth ranging from approximately 15 to 50 feet (5 to 15 m) below the surface. The calf usually positions itself directly below the mother's chin or tucked under a flipper. The calf needs to breathe at shorter intervals than the mother and therefore must rise to the surface alone every few minutes to blow and inhale three or four times while swimming in a circular pattern above its mom. The calf then dives back down to its mother (who may surface every 10–20 minutes). There is frequent touching between mother and calf.

Nursing

Calves have to eat in Hawaii, even though adults do not. Fortunately, their food supply is big, mobile, and always at their side. Humpback calves nurse (that is, they rely entirely on mother's milk) throughout their first winter, and through much of their first year of life. The process of weaning is believed to begin between six and ten months of age on the summer grounds, where more solid food is taken, and ends with separation from the mother after the first feeding season.

Nursing behavior has been observed in Hawaii, with the calf poking its mouth up towards the mother's mammary glands on each side of the genital area on her belly. At times puffs of escaped milk can be seen quickly dissipating into the sea. This activity can occur while the pair are stationary or traveling — clearly a skill that saves on the migration time. However, beyond a handful of underwater encounters with nursing whales, we have no insight into the schedule, duration of bouts, or overall amount of time a mother must spend nursing her calf.

Vulnerability to Boat Collisions

The common humpback mother-and-newborn behavior pattern — of the adult lying stationary beneath the surface for long periods while the calf surfaces alone — makes calves the most likely victims of boat-whale collisions.

With its small profile and almost invisible blows, a calf can be very difficult to spot (even when looking) and especially in any kind of rough sea conditions. Such collisions, causing serious injury to the whale and damage to the boat, occur each year *(see Chapter 7).*

Play

Baby humpbacks play. Mimicry of the mother, or the male escort, is common newborn behavior in Hawaii. Calf surface behaviors, including flippering, spyhops, rolling, tail slaps, tail lashes, tail throws, head lunges, full breaches, and belly flops, are all activities seen in adults *(see Actions and Postures)*.

The calves also play with objects in their environment, such as sticks in a tide-line, boats, or a diver. However, they do not play with each other. The mothers seem to forbid this or, at least, do not allow the circumstances for calves to interact. Whether this has more to do with the mother's reproductive strategy or the calf's survival is not known.

Calves imitated their mothers by repeating the behavior immediately after the mother performed it, including breaching, tail throwing, tail slapping and flippering. They also imitated the escort whale, performing head lunging, throat expansion, chin slapping and bubblestreaming.

Glockner-Ferrari and Ferrari
1985

Calves copy much of the adult behavior around them.

Mothers and calves are relatively quiet (compared to males), but grunt-like sounds have been recorded from calves.

Mother/Calf Communication

When listening (with a hydrophone) near a mother with calf, the over-riding impression is that they are both very quiet! Over the years, single, grunt-like vocalizations from the calf (and in one case loud continuous sounds made by calf, mother or both) have been reported, but these were generally considered exceptional.

A recent study in Hawaii, however, suggests that calf vocalizations may be more common than previously thought. In this project, grunt-like sounds were regularly recorded in both mother/calf and mother/calf/escort groups, and from both male and female calves. The function of the sounds is not known, but suggestions include calling the mother, an alarm call, or a response to something new. There is currently no evidence that the exchange is two-way (that is, returned by the mother).

In contrast to the brash loudness of singers or males in competitive groups, mothers and calves seem to be at the other end of the audio scale. This topic joins the many others awaiting researchers' attention and raises at least three good questions:

- Are mothers and calves indeed relatively quiet, or are we missing something?

- Is quietness a behavior to remain undetected by passing males?

- As the calf is virtually always in physical and/or visual contact with the mother, are calls necessary?

Non-song vocalizations (attributed to the calf) were recorded in 65% of calf pods. These vocalizations were most common in lone mother/calf pairs.

Zoidis et al.
2008

Physical contact is very important between a mother and her newborn. Here a young calf lies on its immobile mother resting at the surface.

JIM DARLING

The Calf And The Escort(s)

In Hawaiian waters, humpback mothers are usually accompanied by a male escort. (The escort role is not that of a father spending time with his offspring.) The specific male in this escort role often changes, either voluntarily as it just ups and departs, through competition for the position (with other males), or when ditched by the female. At times, the escort sings while accompanying the mother and calf. At other times he may pursue the mother. How does the calf relate to all this?

For the most part, it appears the calf is not harmed by all the adult activity. This tentative conclusion comes solely from the observation that such adult action around newborns is very common and there are lots of young calves. So, if a mother finds herself mixed up in a group of males, at least it does not spell sure disaster for the calf. There have been several reports of a calf seemingly ignored when the adults (mother and escort) were otherwise engaged, and others where the calf surfaced alongside the escort rather than its mother — but these are rare, with no indication of the loss or death of the calves or of other negative effects. (However, it should be clear by now that researchers do not see everything that occurs on the breeding grounds.)

The fact is that we have little scientific insight into how the calf is affected by the surrounding social melee. This activity may use up critical energy reserves and even cause injury or, on the other hand, it may play a significant role in calf development and learning. It could be both, with the behavior of the mother around males changing with the age of the calf.

Escorts: Are They Hired Guns?

When a humpback whale mother and calf are alone, they expend a certain amount of energy, when escorted by a single male they expend more energy (as indicated by behavioral changes), and when surrounded by multiple males substantially more energy again. Yet, considering that energy may be the female's most precious asset, the most common social arrangement is the middle option above — the mother, calf, and escort group. Why?

One explanation proposed is that the mother may associate with a single escort as a trade-off — the single escort raises her energy expenditure

Newborn calves spend a lot of their time racing alongside mother just ahead of one or many males. Some speculate that mothers accept a single male escort as he serves to protect her and her newborn from further harassment.

to some degree; however, multiple escorts have the potential for a far greater negative impact. By associating with a single escort, the mother may minimize harassment by other males and the even greater energy expenditure that would entail. This behavior pattern has been described in other mammals with similar female/male associations, and these escort males have been called 'hired guns' or 'bodyguards.'

Is this what is happening in Hawaiian waters? If so, what does the male get out of the arrangement? Does mere presence lead to preference when the female comes into estrus? One twist in the idea is that, as single males also escort a female without a calf, this 'hired gun' behavior (if that is what it is) may be a general female strategy, not just something mothers do.

As escorts join the mother/calf pair, the energy demands increase, especially in the case of multiple escorts versus single escorts.

Cartwright
1999

Juveniles

One segment of the social mix of humpbacks in Hawaiian waters is the juveniles, also referred to as sub-adults. This category includes recently weaned yearlings and whales several years old, before they reach sexual maturity.

There have been no studies focusing on this juvenile 'subculture' of the Hawaiian population. At least some yearlings make their first winter migration to Hawaii with their mothers, and then separate during the breeding assembly. They have little choice but to begin their independent lives in the Islands. Slightly older juvenile whales are also present — presumably having followed the adults during the migration. At the same time, there is evidence that not all juvenile humpbacks make the entire migration.

What insight researchers have on the young animals comes almost entirely from opportunistic observations during studies of mothers and calves or of mature whales involved in mating behavior. The juveniles (usually identified by being bigger than a calf, independent, yet smaller

The juveniles are a little-known segment of the Hawaiian humpback population. Here, a yearling eyes photographer Flip Nicklin.

than an adult) are often found on the periphery of other social groups — following the action but not intimately involved. These smaller whales have specifically been reported:

- Following competitive or surface active groups
- With adult males
- Near adult male/female pairs
- With mother and newborn
- Accompanying each other (in pairs)
- Alone (in one observation, a lone sub-adult was identified as female)

Hints of one behavior pattern of juvenile humpback whales are just beginning to emerge — their interaction with adult males. One study noted two occasions where yearling-sized whales were with an adult male and engaged in apparent sexual activity; at one point the penis of

They (juvenile male and adult male) were rubbing against each other, twirling and swimming upside down and rolling together, 'caressing' each other with their flippers.

Glockner-Ferrari and Ferrari
1985

the sub-adult was extended and rubbed against the genital slit of the adult. There is also an observation where a sub-adult was the apparent object of a fight between adult males. Another study noted a much smaller animal, presumed to be a yearling or a juvenile, with an adult singer.

Other, somewhat incongruous, whale behavior seen in Hawaii is attributed to juveniles. In one case, a juvenile was observed making feeding lunges through a school of mackerel. Also, many of the whales that approach and focus on boats and divers, at times swimming around them for hours, are young animals — likely either intrigued or bored — left out of the more serious activities in the region. All in all, however, the juvenile years (between leaving their mother and becoming sexually mature) are near blank pages in our story of humpback whale society.

Our understanding of young humpback whales is just beginning. Remarkably abundant in some areas during peak season — one comes across mothers and new calves literally every few minutes when boating — their behavior reflects both the necessities of first-year survival as governed by the mother, and the natural play and curiosity of any young mammal. Great questions remain: Where and when are they born? How do they communicate? Why don't they associate with other mothers and new-borns? Are rowdy males a threat to their survival? When weaned, how do they learn to be an adult?

Abundant, healthy humpback whale calves like those we see in Hawaii bode well for the future of this population.

Newborns and Juveniles

Quick Info

When and where do humpback whale births occur?

A humpback whale birth has not been observed. However, there is much circumstantial evidence, including observation of tiny creased calves and placental material, to indicate births occur during the migration and in the winter assembly in Hawaii.

What are the priorities of mother and newborn?

Mothers need to maintain circumstances that are optimal for rest, nursing, and protection of the young, including (at least sometimes) avoidance of sexually active males. Mothers with a newborn maintain separation from breeding activity by staying in shallow waters, just outside reefs.

Why shallow waters?

It is speculated that mothers with young calves stay in shallow waters to avoid sexually active males, rough offshore sea conditions, and/or predators.

Are predators an issue for new mothers?

Killer whales, likely the most formidable predator of humpback whales and common in summer grounds, are rarely seen in Hawaii. However, there are occasional observations of false killer whales (15-ft dolphins) harassing and attacking humpback mothers with a calf. Sharks follow and eat sick or dead whales, but there is no indication they attack healthy animals.

What do newborn humpbacks do?

Newborn humpback whales spend a great deal of time traveling with the mother. They also rest, play, nurse, explore objects in their environment, and stay out of the way when adult males join their mother. Play includes mimicking many of the actions of mother and escort males.

How do the juveniles, who have left mom but are not yet sexually mature, behave?

Knowledge of the behavior of juvenile or sub-adult whales is limited. They are certainly present and often found on the periphery of competitive or other adult groups, or in the company of adult males, including singers. Apparent sexual activity has been observed in these adult male/juvenile groups.

Chapter 7

Whales and Us

The relationship of our modern society with humpback whales has been short but dramatic. After thousands of years of coexistence, we developed the technology that would allow us to catch and kill them en masse. Then, it took us less than a single human lifetime to nearly wipe them from the face of the planet. When whalers could not find any more, they moved on to other, more plentiful, species, and humpback whales were only then protected (in 1966).

Since then, our relationship with whales has swung decidedly in the opposite direction, towards a time of unprecedented interest in the living animal — interest in conservation, research, education, and whale watching. The more we have come to know the whales, the more fascinating they have become, with whales now part of that select group of animals that hold exceptional interest and inspiration for humans.

So what does the future hold? Will the pendulum swing again, as the numbers of humpback whales and their conflicts with human endeavors increase? Have the animals gained a permanent level of respect? Or, regardless of our respect, will depletion of ocean life and marine pollution and traffic have the same impact as whaling? This chapter looks at our relationships with humpback whales — past and present.

How Are Whales Doing?

Arguably, the most common question asked about whales has to do with their status. There is a broad awareness that whales were hunted to near extinction and many are on endangered species lists *(see Appendix)*. There have been decades of high-publicity campaigns to save the whales from the threats of whaling, capture, loss of habitat or prey, collisions, and harassment. However, it is not always clear if these campaigns have been successful, if progress has been made, if the whales are indeed being saved.

For humpbacks, the pendulum has swung from whaling times, when they were seen only as a commodity, to a time of enormous interest in the living animal.

There is no single or simple answer to this question, and certainly not one that applies to the more than 80 species of whales and dolphins. The answer may even be different for populations of the same species living in different parts of the world. Some whales are abundant, some were at endangered levels but with protection numbers are increasing, some are at endangered levels and seem stuck there, and one species has probably become extinct in the last few years. The category a particular population of whales falls into generally depends on the interplay of three things:

- Its recent relationship with humans (if the object of whaling, how many survived).

- Its reproductive potential — how fast they can reproduce.

- The health of its current environment, especially food quality and availability, and the level of pollution.

How Are the 'Hawaiian' Humpback Whales Doing?

The humpback whales off Hawaiian shores currently remain on endangered species lists; however, they have turned the corner in their recovery. All indications are that the numbers in Hawaii, and generally worldwide, have increased steadily since whaling stopped. So, the whales seen in Hawaii are doing well — especially when compared to some other species and populations worldwide. However, to place this statement in context, we need to look at the past, the present, and think about the future of these animals.

Hawaii's humpbacks have recovered well with protection from whaling. This recovery is mirrored in most other humpback whale populations around the world.

Whaling of humpback whales legally ended in 1966, although illegal Soviet whaling continued into the next decade.

The 1900s

Whaling

Through the first sixty or so years of the twentieth century, humpback whale populations were decimated worldwide in one of the greatest massacres of mammals in human history. The North Pacific, and whales we now know as 'Hawaiian' humpbacks, were no exception. The best indication of the efficiency of this hunt was that most whaling operations were abandoned, moved, or switched to other species even before humpback whales were protected internationally in 1966. That is, the most experienced and motivated whale finders in the world — the whalers — could not find any more to hunt.

It is not known how many humpbacks the whalers left in the North Pacific or, for that matter, how many lived in this ocean prior to the onset of whaling. One rough estimate often used is that there were about 15,000 humpback whales in the North Pacific before commercial whaling. Equally rough estimates suggest that 1,200 to 1,400 humpbacks may have survived the whaling operations, or about 10 percent of the pre-whaling numbers. It is important to emphasize the back-of-the-envelope nature of these estimates, and few researchers would be surprised if the actual numbers were double these in both cases. But also, few would argue that the North Pacific humpback whale population was reduced to a small remnant of pre-whaling levels.

Additional humpback whales were still being killed (by the Soviet fleet) in the North Pacific years after international protection in 1966.

Doroshenko
2000

Recovery

Since commercial whaling ended and the species was protected, humpback whales appear to have made a steady comeback in most of their traditional

Evidence of failed harpoon shots are still seen on humpbacks in Hawaiian waters.

JIM DARLING

North Pacific ranges. It is apparent, in the case of North Pacific humpback whales, that a viable population survived the whaling and that their food supply has been adequate over the last few decades. Moreover, as we learned in an earlier chapter, this species has a high reproductive potential — with up to a calf per year for some females. This pattern appears to hold true for many humpback whale populations around the world. We have two concrete signs of this recovery in the North Pacific. (1) Estimates of population size have increased steadily since counts began. And (2) in the last decade or so, humpback whales have re-inhabited traditional ranges around the Pacific Rim empty of the species since whaling times.

The Numbers

- **1970s.** The first estimates of humpback whales in Hawaiian waters suggested a population in the low to mid hundreds. (However, these estimates were based on brief aerial and vessel surveys and could have easily underestimated the population size.)

- **Late 1970s/early 1980s.** The first calculations based on photo-identification of individual whales off Maui produced estimates ranging around 1,000 to 2,000 whales visiting Hawaii over a winter.

- **Early 1990s.** Photo-identification techniques estimated the Hawaiian population at 3,000 to 5,000. A second study (about the same time) estimated 6,000 to 8,000 humpbacks in the entire North Pacific, with 4,000 of those visiting Hawaii.

- **Mid 2000s.** The most recent estimate (developed from an ocean-wide survey known as SPLASH conducted from 2004 to 2006) indicates that approximately 20,000 humpbacks now populate the North Pacific, with half of those visiting Hawaii.

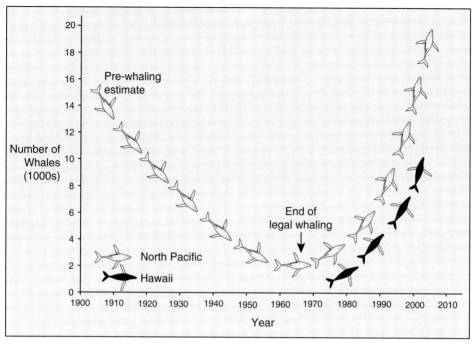

The numbers of humpbacks in Hawaii have increased steadily since whaling stopped. Abundance estimates have gone from a low of 1,000 to 2,000 in the mid-1970s (and first surveys) to 10,000 today. The most recent estimate for the entire North Pacific humpback population is about 20,000 animals. Interpretation of the status of the population (although obviously increasing) is problematic in that the starting-point (or pre-whaling) number of 15,000 shown here was no more than an educated guess.

That is, the numbers of humpback whales in Hawaii have increased steadily from the late 1970s through the 1990s, and into the mid 2000s. In that time, the numbers of humpback whales visiting Hawaii apparently increased at least five-fold. In the last fifteen years alone, the humpback population in Hawaii has doubled.

18,302 represented the best estimate of overall abundance of humpback whales in the North Pacific, excluding calves. Over 50% of this population was estimated to winter in Hawaiian waters.

Calambokidis et al.
2008

Not All Whale Populations Are Recovering

GREG SILBER

North Pacific right whale — Hawaii, 1979

The positive outlook for humpback whales arising from increasing numbers and return to traditional ranges does not, unfortunately, apply to all whales. Certain populations and species remain on the critical list, their future uncertain. Extinction is a real possibility for some. A few examples follow.

- The Yangtze River dolphin, a species that lives only in one river in China, was on a downhill slide for decades due to habitat destruction. Despite conservation efforts, it was declared extinct in 2007.

- The North Pacific right whale (officially protected in 1937) is so rare that a single sighting warrants a scientific publication — it probably numbers only several hundreds. Two sightings of lone right whales have been made in Hawaii in the last thirty years, mixing with humpback whales.

- The North Atlantic right whales (officially protected in 1937), numbering some 300 animals, are living in the midst of major

Western gray whale — Japan, 1993

shipping lanes and fisheries activity, where vessel strikes and entanglements take a critical toll each year.

- The western North Pacific (Asian) gray whales (protected from commercial whaling in 1948) are now represented by a tiny remnant population of about 100 animals with primary feeding grounds overlapping the largest oil and gas development in eastern Asia.

- Other populations of whales at risk, not generally subject to intensive whaling, include killer whales in Washington State and British Columbia and beluga whales in the Gulf of St. Lawrence. These whales are higher on the food chain than the baleen whales and, among other things, are facing increasing health problems from toxins transferred from their industrialized environment.

The simple survival, much less recovery, of these and other whale populations will be an uphill battle.

Hawaiian Humpbacks Today

With a turbulent past behind them, humpback whales in Hawaii are now protected, watched, filmed, studied, and celebrated. They are a topic of school curricula, their songs are broadcast live globally on websites and they are the basis of profitable businesses. They have marine sanctuaries named after them, and are the official state marine mammal of Hawaii. They have both US Federal and Hawaii State government representatives at most whale meetings concerning their protection.

Today, humpback whales in Hawaii (and everywhere else) are an enormous attraction for both the general public and scientists. They are protected, studied, and celebrated.

At the same time, even with all this attention and good will, humpback whales die each year from being entangled in fishing gear and hit by vessels. And these, to be frank, are minor problems when compared to looming threats of renewal of whaling, conflicts over food supply and habitat, or global climate change. The world of humpback whales is anything but secure. For the remainder of this chapter we will look at both the promise and the threats facing humpback whales in the first decades of the twenty-first century.

The Promise — Science And Education

Protection

Humpback whales continue to be protected from whaling by the International Whaling Commission (IWC) and indirectly through a ban on trade of (whaling) products through the Convention on International Trade in Endangered Species of Wild Fauna and Flora (CITES) *(see Appendix)*. (Currently both agreements are being tested by whaling countries.)

Humpback whales are also protected, to varying degrees, by acts or laws of the countries whose boundary waters they visit. The strongest protection is in United States waters with the US Marine Mammal Protection and Endangered Species Acts *(see Appendix)*. Therefore, humpback whales with breeding grounds in Hawaii and feeding grounds in Alaska currently have some of the highest protection of any whales (for that matter of any wildlife) in the world.

There are, however, two caveats regarding present Hawaiian humpback protection. (1) It is not permanent and the whales can be "down-listed" at any time — that is, given reduced protection or taken off protected species lists (this discussion has already begun due to the increase in numbers). (2) When the whales we see in Hawaii travel elsewhere in the Pacific, such as along the Asian coast, the level of protection decreases to, at most, the voluntary IWC agreement not to hunt them (currently indications are this is generally upheld).

Science

As this book testifies, the progress in our scientific understanding of living whales over the last thirty or so years is extraordinary and continuing enthusiastically. The lives and world of these animals are being gradually revealed, as we are literally learning more every day.

There is a steady stream of scientific papers on humpback whales from locations such as Hawaii, Australia, Alaska, the US Eastern Seaboard, the West Indies, Central Africa, Madagascar, Brazil, Ecuador, and others, investigating the whole range of behavioral subjects in this book (as well as other aspects of their biology). Indeed, it is challenging to keep up with the worldwide progress.

The Hawaiian Islands Humpback Whale National Marine Sanctuary

MEAGAN JONES

In 1997, the US and Hawaii governments designated the Hawaiian Islands Humpback Whale National Marine Sanctuary — the nation's twelfth marine sanctuary.

Its purposes are to protect humpback whales and their habitat within the sanctuary; to educate and interpret for the public the relationship of humpback whales and the Hawaiian Islands marine environment; to manage human uses of the sanctuary consistent with the Hawaiian Islands National Marine Sanctuary Act and the National Marine Sanctuary Act; and to identify marine resources and ecosystems of national significance for possible inclusion in the sanctuary.

In fact, humpback whales are currently protected equally inside and outside of the sanctuary boundaries. However, the designation is important symbolically, reflecting the importance of these animals in local and national views.

Research programs worldwide are describing the lives of humpback whales. A student from Italy, in Hawaii for the whale season, ponders spectrographs of song composition.

A search of biological abstracts conducted just before this book went to press listed over 200 papers that include new information on humpback whales published since the year 2000.

Not only is there a growing number of researchers, in more locations, but new technologies are opening doors never dreamed possible a few years ago. It was advances in technology (now seemingly ancient) such as the development of the 35 mm SLR camera and of the hydrophone, in the 1950s and 60s, that led to the first steps in the study of living whales. Now, with sophisticated genetic techniques, satellite tracking, and other 'smart' tags (including placing a camera on the whales themselves), it's clear we have barely begun to achieve what is possible in terms of exploring and understanding the lives of these animals. There is lots of work to do — the field is wide open.

The singer and
his song have
intrigued scientists
(and the public) for
decades.

Education

Whales fascinate us. They capture our imaginations, kids and adults alike, all over the world. The reason is not entirely clear—perhaps it is the combination of the mystery of the unknown oceans, and the unimaginable scale and exceptional grace of the animals. Perhaps it is a result of Jules Verne's *20,000 Leagues Under the Sea* and Herman Melville's *Moby Dick*, or Jacques Cousteau and the *National Geographic* photographs and films of wild whales, where reality has indeed proven more incredible than the fantasy of the early works. Whatever the reasons, they have been compelling to our species.

There is an insatiable desire worldwide for popular and educational materials featuring whales: articles and books, radio and TV shows, school curricula, and community whale festivals. Humpback whales, due to their regular appearance in nearshore locales such as Hawaii combined with their propensity for surface behavior and acrobatics that attract our attention, are one of the best-known whales and the subject of much global media attention.

Most importantly, and as any educator will attest, this interest in whales is often the key to the introduction to other marine life and environmental issues. And it even leads a few to careers in marine research and conservation.

Whales are the perfect catalyst for marine-education programs. Kids from Maui schools enthusiastically recreate a humpback's tail markings (used for individual photo-identification) on life-sized tails (measured during a research program). This took place at Whale Quest Kapalua, a public event on Maui.

JASON A. MOORE

JIM DARLING

Whale watching is a hugely successful industry and a powerful economic argument against whaling. It also provides an opportunity for increasing public awareness of our oceans and the issues and challenges ahead.

Whale Watching

Whale watching, now huge, began modestly in the 1950s in California when a few boats went to watch gray whales migrate along the coast. It has since grown into a worldwide industry, existing in virtually every country with a coastline.

The latest statistics on whale watching are now about ten years old. At the end of the 1990s, whale watching was responsible for a global income estimated at over one billion dollars annually, with nine million clients in eighty-seven countries and territories, in 492 communities. In Hawaii during the 1998–99 season, for instance, fifty-two boats took out 370,000 passengers, with $11.2 million in ticket sales alone; with peripheral sales, income was an estimated $20 million.

Whale watching is not only popular and profitable. It also provides a powerful economic argument for the sustainable use of living whales versus killed whales (and their one-time use as meat and fertilizer). Whale watching has become a significant factor in the economic survival and growth of small coastal communities around the world.

Whale watching also has enormous unquantifiable benefits as a medium of awareness, education, and experience. Perhaps the most significant contribution in the long run is that it draws millions of people to the ocean and introduces them to two-thirds of our planet — something that would otherwise be an unlikely occurrence for many. A close encounter with a wild whale is enthralling, inspiring, and rather than satiating, often leads to more trips, more locations, a desire to see different species and behavior, and to learn more about our oceans.

Approaching Whales in Hawaii

Federal and State regulations prohibit any unauthorized approach to humpback whales in the Hawaiian Islands within 100 yards (90 m) on the water and below 1,000 feet (305 m) in the air.

Researchers that make closer approaches as part of their studies require both Federal (National Marine Fisheries Service) and Hawaii State (Department of Land and Natural Resources) permits.

Researchers must fly yellow flags with permit numbers from their boats, or if working from aircraft, must have contacted enforcement personnel prior to the activity.

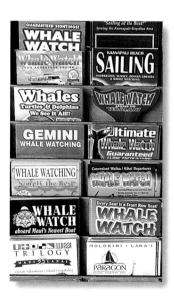

Humpbacks die each year entangled in fishing and mooring gear. In Hawaii, some of those entangled are freed, but not all can be reached or saved.

The Threats

Even with humpbacks making a healthy recovery, there are enormous challenges ahead in the conservation and management of this (and all wild) species. All have to do with the consequences of human development and/or commerce — that is, conflicts, directly or indirectly, with human activities. Following are a few issues discussed daily in whale research and conservation circles, divided into threats to individuals and threats to populations overall.

Threats to Individuals: Entanglements and Collisions

Today, the mostly likely threats to an otherwise healthy humpback whale involve entanglements with fishing gear and collisions with vessels — both on the rise as whale populations recover.

These entanglement and/or collision threats generally affect individuals more than the population overall. This is not meant to downplay the issue in any way, as they are clearly traumatic, painful, and/or deadly to that animal. However, these are threats that affect one individual at a time versus those that can affect the viability of a population in general, as discussed below.

It is worth noting that, in highly endangered whale populations, the death of just one individual — particularly a mature female — can have a significant impact on the health of the entire population, so these threats should not be taken lightly.

Entanglements

It is not known how many humpback whales are lost to entanglements with fishing and mooring gear each year. Certainly, every season, entangled whales are found in Hawaii. As this location is the furthest from the greatest overlap between whales and intensive fishing activity (in their summer grounds), it's likely these are a small segment of those afflicted.

At times, the entangled whales are located and cut free, a service currently conducted by the Hawaiian Islands Humpback Whale National Marine Sanctuary personnel. At other times, the whales move out of range and/or the damage is so severe they will not recover. Most of the entanglements are net or line wrapped around the flukes, flippers, or head; on occasion, the whales are actually towing mooring buoys. The sources of the problem are active fishing operations, as well as the tons of discarded and lost gear and garbage floating at sea.

From 2002 to 2008, as many as 35 different humpback whales were found entangled (in fishing gear, marine debris, mooring systems) in Hawaii.

Lyman and Mattila
2008

Two sets of the fishing gear removed from whales in Hawaii were traced back to crab/cod pot gear used in the Aleutian Islands.

Lyman and Mattila
2007

Vessel–Whale Collisions

Each year collisions between vessels and humpback whales occur throughout their range. These often result in the injury or death of the whale, and significant damage to the vessel.

The number of collisions reported in Hawaii in winter is increasing, and it is likely these are only a portion of those that actually occur. (The increase in reports may be partially due to improved record keeping in recent years.) The density of the whales in peak season can be so great that it is amazing collisions are not more frequent. In most cases, the whale is not seen again, so the extent of its injuries is not known. In other cases, it is clear the whale is bleeding and in serious trouble.

The most likely whale victims in Hawaii are the newborn calves, which must surface several times to mother's once. These small calves are easy to miss, even when watching for them, if moving at typical

Newborn humpbacks are especially vulnerable to collisions with vessels, as is illustrated by this calf sliced by a boat propeller. Such collisions are on the increase.

vessel speeds of 20 knots or more. Other whale victims are those sleeping motionless on or just under the surface, apparently only semi-conscious.

The solution is low tech — lower speed in the areas of high whale density. This would solve much of the problem, but is not currently regulated; indeed, in Hawaii just the opposite is happening with the introduction of high-speed super ferries between the main islands.

During the 2006–07 winter season, there were at least six confirmed collisions between boats and whales in Hawaii; in the 2007–08 season there were 12 reported ship-strikes.

Schofield
2007, 2008

With numbers of humpback whales increasing, they have the full attention of whaling interests. More whales will also inevitably result in more conflicts with human activity.

Threats to Populations: Hunting, Food, and Habitat

Population-scale threats tend to affect more than one whale at a time, and may weaken or destroy an entire population or even species. Humpback whales have in their favor the strengths of being a global species, being flexible about food type, and having a high reproductive rate. With these assets, humpbacks may be able to biologically dodge and weave their way through some of these threats for a time, but without human intervention on their behalf, eventually the viability of populations will be compromised.

Commercial Whaling

Currently, there is no legal whaling of humpback whales in the North Pacific. However, this is a temporary state, with no guarantee that whaling will not occur in the future. The whaling interests are alive and well and waiting, taking every opportunity to re-establish the industry in locations and with species not considered as endangered as humpback whales — and humpback whales are on the verge of losing their endangered status. With growing human populations, and the collapse of traditional fisheries around the world, it would be naïve to think these animals will not again be targeted.

A count of endangered humpback whales is revealing a comeback so convincing that marine scientists are pondering the controversial question: Is it time for the whales, hunted to near-extinction in the 20th century, to have less protection . . .

San Jose Mercury News
June 8, 2007

The Down-Listing and Whaling Debate

Due to the increase in numbers of humpback whales in the North Pacific, the debate has begun as to whether or not they should be taken off endangered species lists — that is, down-listed to a lesser level of protection. Among other things, this decision to down-list would make a renewal of whaling much easier.

Most researchers view this situation with mixed emotions. Endangered species acts and laws are based only on numbers (not on how much we know about the animals and their biological requirements). On one hand, it's very positive that the numbers of humpback whales have increased, and few would argue that the endangered designation should be for truly endangered species. On the other hand, should this rise in numbers mean that humpbacks are all of a sudden fair game?

JIM DARLING

Humpback whales engulf masses of small fish with great efficiency (by expanding throat pleats to create a huge maw, as shown above). Conflicts with human fisheries may be unavoidable in the future.

Competition with Human Fisheries

Humans and humpback whales share some of the same prey, including such species as herring and sardines (pilchards). Currently, in the case of North Pacific humpback whales and fishermen, there is apparently enough to go around, but will this overlap be a factor in the future of the whales? Odds are the answer is yes, in one or more of the following ways:

- With increasing numbers of whales and reduced fish stocks, the whales and fishermen compete in the same areas, with entanglement in gear an issue.

- The over-fishing and disappearance of fish stocks, of which there are many examples, force the whales to move to other regions or species that may be less than optimal.

- Whales are blamed for the reduction in fish stocks as a justification to renew whaling.

All three of these scenarios are occurring today to some extent. The last of these is an ongoing debate at the IWC, with the whaling factions arguing relentlessly that the whales are eating all "our" fish — so we need to hunt them. There is no scientific basis for this claim, but it is not unusual for us to blame other species for fishery troubles — particularly a species that is perceived as having more commercial value dead than alive.

Humpback whales range over such large (and often remote) areas that it is nearly impossible to document potential problems, much less monitor them. Below, humpbacks feed amongst thousands of seabirds in the Bering Sea.

Human activities and pollution are altering the environment of whales. These range from overt acts such as harmful military sonar, to a myriad of more subtle and long- term actions that may affect habitat and food supply.

Changing Natural Habitats: Pollution to Climate Change

Human activities are changing the habitats of whales in myriad ways, ranging from increasing marine traffic, to industrial development, to chemical and noise pollution, to climate change. These will have an impact on whales either directly through destruction of habitat or indirectly through influences on their prey.

In a few cases, the causes of lethal impacts are blatantly obvious — such as the loss of the Yangtze River dolphin to river industry (one observer likened it to dolphins trying to live on the median of a free-way), belugas in the Gulf of St. Lawrence dying of diseases directly linked to pollutant chemicals, or naval sonar activities leading to whale strandings.

In most cases, though, it can be extremely difficult to recognize and measure the non-lethal impacts of habitat pollution and change. Our limited knowledge of natural behavior patterns makes it hard to identify critical changes, and the huge, multinational ranges many whales travel over make it impossible to be aware of all the circumstances they encounter. So, by the time a whale strands (or dies), it is often too late to do much about it as the causes may be too far away in time and/or location.

In Hawaii, a few examples of habitat change are increasing vessel traffic (including fast ferries that speed through breeding grounds), run-off from agricultural lands clouding near-shore waters, harbor construction, and naval exercises that include use of strikingly loud sonar sounds. Remember, however, that most individual whales are only present in Hawaii for several weeks before returning to feeding grounds where other habitat issues dog both them and their prey.

Cumulative Impacts — Adding Them All Together

Many small changes to whale behavior, themselves insignificant, may accumulate and develop into a significant threat. Seemingly minor impacts may include a whale researcher disturbing a whale for a few minutes, then a whale-watch boat, then the noise of a passing tugboat and barge, a near miss of a ferry, slightly less food due to a fishing operation, having to swim around (or get entangled in) a discarded fishing net, then moving away from an area due to tolerable but bothersome noise levels. The concern is that these cumulative impacts may affect the health of the individual over time through stress-related disease and/or more energy expenditure and less energy input than is optimal.

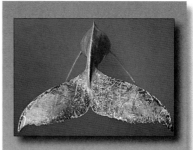

Extreme Noise Pollution: Naval Active Sonar Systems

Military active sonar emits intense sound waves that travel through tens to hundreds of miles of ocean to locate enemy submarines. Such capability requires an extremely loud sound source — so loud that it changes the behavior of whales, and can even result in their injury and death.

Some toothed whales appear to be especially sensitive to these sound levels, with multiple examples of strandings, bleeding from brain and ears, and death documented worldwide.

The impact of these sounds on baleen whales, including humpback whales, is less clear. One study was conducted in Hawaii to determine the impact of naval sonar (at less than full strength) on humpback whales. Whereas no immediate stranding or deaths occurred, the sounds did change behavior, causing some whales to stop singing and other whales to lengthen their song during sonar playback.

Climate Change

JIM DARLING

There is now no doubt that pollution from human technology is changing ecological systems worldwide. The ultimate impacts that global warming will have on specific species like humpback whales are near impossible to predict due to the complexity of ocean systems. However, a rise of only a few degrees in ocean temperature could affect humpback whales by causing, for example:

- Changes in ocean circulation and thus plankton and the overall food web. Humpback whales are doing well with the status quo, so any change will undoubtedly impact them in some way.

- Movement of the whales away from the Hawaiian Islands so as to stay within the apparent optimal range of water temperature they seek during winter.

- Disruption of the primary food of potential predators like the killer whale or false killer whale, thereby forcing them to target humpback whales more than occurs today.

One of the reasons biologists are so concerned about this problem is that we have no idea of the outcome. It is a cliché now, but this is truly a global experiment with all species the subjects. Change is the only sure result, with the final stable state anyone's guess.

So, Why Don't We Just Protect Whales?

There are three substantial human forces defining, or trying to define, our relationship with whales today.

There are the whaling interests, which view whales as a commodity. These include factions in countries such as Japan and Norway, with abstinence-type assistance — that is, no objection — from other countries. These factions are well-funded, sophisticated, and determined to resume whaling operations.

Second are the ocean-based industries and activities, including fisheries, oil exploitation, and military, that increasingly find themselves in conflict over space and resources used by whales. These industries rarely (if ever) want to harm the whales, but the animals are in the way of activity deemed more important. Pollution, habitat loss, noise, entanglements, and cumulative effects are all issues.

A third, and potentially very powerful, positive force is the collective voice of people who recognize the value of protecting whales and their habitat — whether it be for maintaining a culture, making a living, teaching our kids, or better understanding our planet. This force is rooted in people who have come to realize that healthy whale populations, while desirable in and of themselves, also reflect a healthy world.

These forces meet on a regular basis. The whales, and critical ocean habitat, don't always win. Perhaps the greatest threat to humpback whales (and true for all wildlife) is our lack of understanding of their ecological and social requirements — what these animals really need to stay alive and healthy. Without this knowledge, the best intentions are unlikely to solve the conflicts that are inevitable. This is the challenge for researchers and educators.

What's Next For Humpbacks?

Few experienced biologists would dare predict the future of complex natural systems and the species they support. We have learned on one hand of their fragility and, on the other, of their flexibility, adaptability, and resilience. However, one would be hard pressed to find examples of any large wild animal found to be in conflict with human endeavor, or seen as a commercial commodity, that is far from jeopardy. This makes the future of humpback whales particularly tenuous.

We are in the midst of an era when humpback whales have received the best of human attention. They are recovering globally and, unlike some other whale species, the potential for healthy wild populations may still exist. Humpback whales, in regions like Hawaii, have returned our favor in spades. They have helped bring conservation issues home to us. They have supported our livelihoods, inspired our science, art, music, and literature. They have charged the imaginations of our kids. They have made us want to know more about the world we live in — from diatom to copepod, to sardine, to whale.

The decision to stop whaling allowed the recovery of humpback whales, and many populations are thriving, but this relatively peaceful time is likely not permanent.

However, the jury (that is, us) that will determine their future is still out. On one hand, there has never been more human energy directed towards research, public awareness, and conservation. On the other, the fundamental problems whales face — pollution and habitat loss and whaling due to growth of human populations, industry, and markets — have not gone away, are not being resolved, and indeed are growing. The conservation of humpback whales, as with other wild species, will depend entirely on: (1) the will to act; and (2) acquiring the knowledge to act wisely. Neither, alone, will protect the whales.

Today, humpback whales are in a relative calm — between commercial whaling, and the potential destruction of the natural systems that support them (along with probably more whaling). During this period there is the urgency to learn as much as we can about whales — to actually understand their environmental and social requirements, to recognize their value as living animals, and to work to protect them.

We are literally dipping our
toes into the world of humpback
whales, with the promise of many
more insights and discoveries
awaiting us.

Whales and Us

Quick Info

Are humpback whales in Hawaii recovering?

Humpback whales in Hawaii, and in many regions worldwide, are recovering relatively well (compared to some other whale species), with numbers increasing steadily since whaling ended.

What laws protect them?

Humpback whales are protected from whaling internationally through the IWC (International Whaling Commission) and from illegal trade by CITES (Convention on International Trade in Endangered Species of Wild Fauna and Flora). In addition, the United States has strong laws — the Marine Mammal Protection Act and the Endangered Species Act — that protect these animals in US waters.

What are the greatest current threats to the humpback whales seen in Hawaii?

The greatest current, day-to-day threats to these whales are entanglements with fishing gear or marine garbage and collisions with vessels.

Do we know enough about humpback whales to provide meaningful management in conflicts with industry or renewed whaling?

Unfortunately, no. While our knowledge of humpback whales is greater than for many other whale species, our understanding of their habitat, food, social, and behavioral requirements is not yet adequate to manage major conflicts with humans.

What does the future look like for humpback whales?

As human population and industry expand, it is very likely conflicts with whales (and with all wildlife) will increase. The whalers are standing by. One safe prediction is that the goal of conserving healthy populations of whales will become increasingly challenging in the future.

Appendix

Agreements and Laws Protecting Humpback Whales

INTERNATIONAL

The International Whaling Commission (IWC)

The IWC was established in 1946 with the purpose of providing "the proper conservation of whale stocks, and thus make possible the orderly development of the whaling industry." As is clearly stated, conservation is only part of its mandate — and this is for the purpose of continued whaling. However, the IWC is the only international management forum for whales — it is the organization that officially protected humpback whales and other species, designated sanctuaries, and set whaling limits and seasons. There are seventy-seven member nations. Critically, no government is bound by any IWC regulation if it chooses to object.

Convention on International Trade in Endangered Species of Wild Fauna and Flora (CITES)

CITES is a 1975 international agreement between governments whose purpose is to ensure that international trade in specimens of wild animals and plants does not threaten their survival. It accords varying degrees of protection to more than 30,000 species of animals and plants. Humpback whales are one of these species. The way it works is that, if one country flaunts international agreement not to hunt the whales, they cannot sell the products legally to another country. There are currently 172 countries that are members, but similar to the IWC, adherence to the agreement is voluntary. Each member country adopts its own domestic legislation to ensure that CITES is implemented at the national level.

NATIONAL

In US Waters

Marine Mammal Protection Act (MMPA) 1972

All marine mammals are protected under the MMPA. The MMPA prohibits, with certain exceptions, the take of marine mammals in US waters and by US citizens on the high seas, and the importation of marine mammals and marine mammal products into the US.

Endangered Species Act (ESA) 1973

The Endangered Species Act provides for the conservation of species that are endangered or threatened throughout all or a significant portion of their range, and the conservation of the ecosystems on which they depend.

A species is considered *endangered* if it is in danger of extinction throughout all or a significant portion of its range. A species is considered *threatened* if it is likely to become an endangered species within the foreseeable future.

The definition of *take* (which in turn defines what these Acts mean to whales) is slightly different between the two Acts.

- *Take* under the MMPA means to "harass, hunt, capture, kill or collect, or attempt to harass, hunt, capture, kill or collect."

- *Take* under the ESA means "to harass, harm, pursue, hunt, shoot, wound, kill, trap, capture, or collect, or to attempt to engage in any such conduct."

Special permits are required to potentially "take," that is, "harass," whales during research operations. As regards research, any disturbance that changes natural behavior (however slightly) is considered a "take."

Hawaii State Regulations

The Hawaii State Department of Land and Natural Resources (DLNR) manages aquatic species in Hawaiian waters, including humpback whales. They work in collaboration with federal departments in enforcing Hawaiian humpback whale protection regulations, and require state permits (in addition to the Federal NMFS permits) for any activity that may contravene the regulations.

In Canadian Waters

Humpback whales seen in Hawaii in the winter may spend the summer feeding season in waters under Canadian jurisdiction, along the British Columbia coastline.

Cetacean Protection Regulations (1982)

Cetacean Protection Regulations, issued under the Fisheries Act, require that anyone, other than Indians and Inuit, wishing to hunt cetaceans must obtain a license from the Minister of Fisheries before doing so. Indians and Inuit are allowed to hunt all cetaceans, except "right whales" (balaenids), without a license if the products are used for local consumption.

The Cetacean Protection Regulations prohibit any form of harassment of cetaceans, including repeated attempts to pursue, disperse, herd whales and any repeated intentional act or negligence resulting in the disruption of their normal behavior.

Species at Risk Act (SARA) 2003

This Act provides for further protection of species considered at risk. Currently North Pacific humpback whales are categorized as "threatened" under this Act.

Among other things, this Act makes it an offence to kill, harm, harass, capture, or take an individual that is extirpated, endangered, or threatened; possess, collect, buy, sell, or trade an individual of a listed species or its part or derivative; damage or destroy the residence of one or more individuals of a listed species.

When Hawaiian Humpbacks
Are Not in US or Canadian Waters

Hawaiian humpback whales migrate through, and range into, inter-national waters as well as the national waters of other North Pacific Rim countries. Protection in these waters relies on agreements (non-binding) made at the IWC and CITES as discussed above.

Glossary

agonistic All aspects of aggression, including threats and actual attack, appeasement, and flight.

allomaternal Care-giving of an infant by an animal other than its mother.

anecdote A short personal account of an incident or event.

artiodactyls An order of mammals, the even-toed ungulates (hoofed animals), that includes cows, sheep, and antelope. They share a common evolutionary ancestor with whales.

baleen whales Whales that, instead of teeth, have a filtering system in their mouth made out of keratin plates called baleen.

birth rate Average number of offspring produced by a female over a given time.

blowhole Nostrils of a whale through which they inhale and exhale. Baleen whales have two blowholes side by side — toothed whales have only one.

breach *See Actions and Postures*

breath-holders Whale research jargon usually referring to a pair of adult whales that spend long periods underwater and little time on the surface.

bubblestream *See Actions and Postures*

cetaceans The order of mammals that includes whales, dolphins, and porpoises.

CITES Convention on International Trade in Endangered Species of Wild Fauna and Flora, an international agreement to prevent countries trading in products of endangered species.

competitive behavior Interactions between animals striving for the same, mutually exclusive, goal.

conservation The protection of living plants and animals and their habitats.

cooperative behavior Behavior involving individuals working together (helping each other) towards a goal.

copepod Small (mostly planktonic) animals that are a major source of protein in oceans and important to whales both directly as prey and as a critical component of marine food webs.

Cousteau, Jacques French filmmaker who popularized ocean exploration and conservation through his TV programs in the 1960s and 70s.

cumulative effects A number of small impacts that combine to create a greater impact.

diatom Unicellular (one-celled) algae (phytoplankton) that are the basis of many marine food webs.

Discovery tag Metal dart once shot into a living whale to be recovered at time of death (from whaling) to determine its movements.

dominance hierarchy Social hierarchy (in animals often determined by physical differences) where certain individuals control the distribution of available resources (e.g. receptive females).

down-list The reassignment of a species from a higher to a lower category of protection (e.g. from "endangered" to "threatened," or from "threatened" to "recovered").

echolocation A method in which an animal emits pulses of sound and listens to the echoes to determine location, range, and nature of objects in the environment for navigation and feeding.

epimeletic Helping behavior; in cetaceans it often involves healthy individual(s) helping sick or injured ones.

escort An adult male humpback whale that accompanies a mother with calf, and that will defend his position against other males.

estrus The period when a female is sexually receptive, when eggs are produced and, with mating, pregnancy is most likely to occur.

extant A species or group of organisms that still exists, that is not extinct.

extinct A species or group of organisms that no longer exists.

Feresa (Pygmy Killer Whale) A slender black dolphin with distinctive white lips less than ten feet (3 m) in length, widely distributed in tropical waters.

fertilization The fusion of sperm and egg that leads to an embryo (and offspring).

fitness In biology, the ability of an organism to transfer its genes to the next generation.

flipper Fin on the forward sides of the whale; in humpbacks they are long and wing-like.

gene Fundamental unit that contains genetic information determining the characteristics of a living organism.

genetic diversity The range of genes within a species.

gestation The development of the embryo in mammals. The gestation period is the time between fertilization of the egg and birth.

GPS Standard short form of Global Positioning System, which provides exact longitude and latitude position determined by satellite.

Greenpeace One of the first grassroots organizations to protest whaling in the 1970s.

habitat A part of the environment that is occupied by a specific plant or animal species.

headknobs Distinctive knobs on the top of the head of humpback whales (formally called tubercules). Each knob has a hair in it that may have a sensory function.

herring A small fish (< 15 in / 40 cm) that lives in vast schools in oceans of the northern hemisphere; it is an important prey for whales.

hydrophone An underwater microphone (used to detect whale sounds).

hypothesis A potential explanation based on observations of a phenomenon or behavior that is not yet fully understood.

IWC The International Whaling Commission, an international organization that manages whaling and therefore influences whale conservation.

joiner A common research term for a lone adult whale (male) that joins a singing humpback whale.

juvenile A young whale that has separated from its mother but is not yet sexually mature.

killer whale (*Orcinus orca*) Largest of the dolphin family (15–30 ft, or 5–10 m). Found in all oceans; top oceanic predator that may include large whales in its diet.

krill A small, shrimp-like marine animal (a type of zooplankton called a euphausiid) that is an important food source for some baleen whales.

lactation Production of milk from the mammary glands by the adult female mammal in order to suckle its young.

lee The side sheltered from the wind, usually due to high land acting as a windbreak.

lek Gathering of males for purposes of competitive mating display.

mammary glands Glands in female mammals that produce milk for suckling young.

migration Cyclical movements that occur during the life of an animal at definite intervals. In humpback whales, migration occurs between summer feeding and winter breeding grounds.

Mysticeti The sub-order of cetaceans that includes the baleen whales.

non-agonistic Used to refer to behavior patterns that are not aggressive in nature.

nursery Specific location where young animals are found.

Odontoceti The sub-order of cetaceans that includes the toothed whales.

operational sex ratio Ratio of number of mature males to number of sexually receptive females available at any given time during the breeding season.

ovaries That part of the female reproductive system that produces eggs.

ovulation The release of the egg from the ovary into the oviduct, where it may be fertilized.

peduncle Area of a whale's body just forward of the tail (also referred to as the tail stock).

photogrammetry Photographic technique to determine the size of an object.

photo-identification (photo-ID) Identification of individual animals by photographs of natural markings.

photo-ID matches Repeat sightings of the same individual whale determined by matching identification photographs taken at different times.

placenta Point of attachment of embryo to mother and through which the embryo is nourished.

population Total individuals of one species that inhabit a particular locality or region.

post-partum estrus Estrus that occurs shortly after giving birth.

Pseudorca (False Killer Whale) Black dolphin up to about fifteen feet (5 m) in length, widely distributed in warm temperate waters and tropical waters. Potential predator of humpback whales.

reproductive strategy Life history or behavior that results in greater survival and reproductive success.

sardine A small fish (also known as a pilchard) living in huge schools and an important food to whales.

satellite tag Electronic tag attached to a whale that sends location signals to a satellite to allow tracking over extended times and distances.

scientific process Testing a hypothesis by means of experiments designed to either support or invalidate it.

seasonally polyestrus A term used to describe a female that has multiple estrus cycles during a specific time of year.

sexual maturity Age when an individual animal can reproduce.

social sounds Sounds made by humpback whales that are not song, that is, not repeated in a cyclical pattern.

song In biology, a series of sounds that are repeated over and over. Humpback whale males sing a complex, ever-changing song.

spermatogenesis Sperm production in the male.

SPLASH Acronym for a study on the abundance and status of North Pacific humpback whales from 2004 to 2006, termed Structure of Population Levels of Abundance and Status of Humpback Whales.

sub-population A portion of the entire population often defined by a particular characteristic (e.g. all juvenile humpbacks in Hawaii).

surface active group (SAG) (or competitive group) An often fast-moving group of multiple males and one female characterized by competition between the males over access to the female.

tail fluke Each side of a whale's tail.

tail stock Area of a whale's body just forward of the tail, also called a peduncle.

testes That part of the male reproductive system that produces sperm.

throat pleats Pleats in the underside of a whale's throat that allow the throat to greatly expand when taking in mouthfuls of food or in displays.

tiger shark A large predatory shark (to 14 ft, or 4.25 m) common around islands in the central Pacific; it eats almost anything.

toothed whale A whale with teeth, including the sperm whale, killer whales, and all dolphins and porpoises (sub-order Odontoceti).

zooplankton Small animals that float in ocean currents; they are a major food source for baleen whales.

Actions and Postures

Humpback whales engage in specific actions and postures while involved in the behavior patterns described in this book. In many cases, several different terms are used to describe the same activity, as different research groups coined the terms. Below, the most common term is listed first with alternatives in parentheses.

The actions and postures that occur in a variety of social situations, by both sexes (or sex specificity not confirmed), and throughout the year, are described first. Other activities, primarily (but not exclusively) performed by males when competing for females are presented separately below.

Occur in a Variety of Social Situations

Side Fluke *(half fluke, lateral fluke display)*
Whale is at the water surface with one fluke blade extended above the surface as it swims on its side.

Inverted Posture *(belly-up)*
Whale turns ventral side towards the surface.

Roll
The whale rolls ventral side or belly-up, at times slapping flippers on the surface as it rolls all the way over.

Head Rise *(spy hop)*
Whale raises its head vertically out of the water while stationary with flippers outstretched (without open mouth or extended throat pleats).

Tail Extension
Whale raises its tail slowly into the air, usually high enough that the genital area is above the surface, and holds it there for a time.

Tail Arch
The whale arches and curves its tail stock and fluke into an "S" shape on the horizontal plane and holds it there while swimming forward.

Flippering *(flipper slap)*
The whale raises a flipper into the air and slaps it down on the water surface once or many (20+) times in succession.

Tail Lob *(lob tail, fluke slap)*
The whale slaps its tail on the surface, either right-way-up (slapping the underside of its flukes) or belly-up (slapping dorsal surface of its flukes).

Rear Body Throw *(tail throw, peduncle slap)*
The whale throws the rear portion of its body from the water, often twisting to land on its side.

Belly-Flop *(half breach)*
The whale leaps partially out of the water and lands on its belly.

Breach
The whale leaps from the water, spinning in the air before re-entry. Two associated whales may breach simultaneously (double breach).

Occur Primarily in Competitive Groups of Males

Tail Lash *(fluke swish)*
One whale lashes its tail, often towards another. Can occur with flukes on a horizontal or vertical plane.

Head Lunge
The whale lunges forward with most of its head coming out of the water.

Underwater Blow
The whale releases a blast of air from its blowhole below the surface of the water, often just prior to surfacing.

Bubblestream *(bubble trail)*
The submerged whale releases a controlled stream of bubbles from its blowhole, leaving a trail behind it.

Air Gulp *(throat inflation)*
The whale gulps air, greatly extending its throat pleats. It releases the air underwater.

Head Slap *(chin slap)*
Whale lunges/leaps partially out of the water and strikes the ventral side of its head forcefully on the surface.

Head Lift
The whale swims with its back arched and head above the surface.

Jaw Clap
The whale opens and closes its jaws, clapping them together, at times audibly.

Chasing *(tail chasing)*
One whale rapidly chases another. The leader may throw its tail upward with the chaser lunging behind.

Charge
One whale charges at another, often bubblestreaming in the process.

Block
One whale blocks the path of another with its body.

Strike
One whale intentionally strikes another with its flukes, whether underwater or on the surface.

Collision
Two whales collide, apparently intentionally.

Trumpeting
A whale vocalizes on the surface with a prolonged, low, foghorn-like sound emitted from the blowhole.

References

Amos, W. 1997. Marine mammal tissue sample collection and preservation for genetic analysis. In *Molecular genetics of marine mammals*. eds. A. Dizon, S. Chivers, and W. Perrin, 107–116. Lawrence, KS: The Society for Marine Mammalogy.

Au, W. W., L. J. Mobley, W. C. Burgess, M. O. Lammers, and P. E. Nachtigall. 2000. Seasonal and diurnal trends of chorusing humpback whales wintering in waters off western Maui. *Marine Mammal Science* 16:530–544.

Baker, C. S. 1985. The population structure and social organization of humpback whales (*Megaptera novaeangliae*) in the central and eastern North Pacific. PhD diss., Univ. of Hawaii, Honolulu.

Baker, C. S., and L. M. Herman. 1981. Migration and local movement of humpback whales in Hawaiian waters. *Canadian Journal of Zoology* 59:460–469.

———. 1984. Aggressive behavior between humpback whales (*Megaptera novaeangliae*) wintering in Hawaiian waters. *Canadian Journal of Zoology* 62:1922–1937.

———. 1984. Seasonal contrasts in the social behavior of the humpback whale. *Cetus* 5:14–16.

———. 1987. Alternative population estimates of humpback whales (*Megaptera novaeangliae*) in Hawaiian waters. *Canadian Journal of Zoology* 65:2818–2821.

Baker, C. S., L. M. Herman, A. Perry, W. S. Lawton, J. M. Straley, A. A. Wolman, G. D. Kaufman, H. E. Winn, J. D. Hall, J. M. Reinke, and J. Ostman. 1986. Migratory movement and population structure of humpback whales (*Megaptera novaeangliae*) in the central and eastern North Pacific. *Marine Ecology Progress Series* 31:105–119.

Baker, C. S., A. Perry, and L. M. Herman. 1987. Reproductive histories of female humpback whales, *Megaptera novaeangliae*, in the North Pacific. *Marine Ecology Progress Series* 41:103–114.

Barlow, J. 2006. Cetacean abundance in Hawaiian waters estimated from a summer/fall survey in 2002. *Marine Mammal Science* 22:446–464.

Barlow, J., and P. J. Clapham. 1996. A new birth interval approach to estimating demographic parameters of humpback whales. *Ecology* 78:535–545.

Bauer, G. H. 1986. The behavior of humpback whales in Hawaii and modification of behavior induced by human intervention. PhD diss., Univ. of Hawaii, Honolulu.

Bermuda Zoological Society. 1983. Frank Watlington. *Newsletter of the Bermuda Zoological Society* 6:1 & 5.

Best, P. B., J. L. Bannister, R. L. Brownell, and G. P. Donovan, eds. 2001. Right whales: Worldwide status. Special Issue 2, *Cetacean Research and Management*.

Bigg, M. A., I. B. MacAskie, and G. Ellis. 1976. *Abundance and movement of killer whales off eastern and southern Vancouver Island with comments on management*. Unpublished report. Nanaimo, BC: Pacific Biological Station. Canada.

Brown, M., and P. Corkeron. 1995. Pod characteristics of migrating humpback whales (*Megaptera novaeangliae*) off the east Australian coast. *Behavior* 132:163–179.

Brown, M. R., P. J. Corkeron, P. T. Hale, K. W. Schultz, and M. M. Bryden. 1995. Evidence for a sex segregated migration in the humpback whale (*Megaptera novaeangliae*). *Proceedings Royal Society London Series* B 259:229–234.

Calambokidis, J., E. A. Falcone, T. J. Quinn, A. M. Burdin, P. J. Clapham, J. K. F. Ford, C. M. Gabriele, R. LeDuc, D. Mattila, L. Rojas-Bracho, J. M. Straley, B. Taylor, J. Urban, D. Weller, B. H. Witteveen, M. Yamaguchi, A. Bendlin, D. Camacho, K. Flynn, A. Havron, J. Huggins, and N. Maloney. 2008. SPLASH: Structure of Population Levels of Abundance and Status of Humpback Whales in the North Pacific. Final Report U.S. Dept. of Commerce Contract AB133F-03-RP-00078 Seattle, WA: Cascadia Research, Olympia, WA.

Calambokidis, J., G. H. Steiger, J. M. Straley, L. M. Herman, S. Cerchio, D. R. Salden, J. Urban R., J. K. Jacobsen, O. von Zeigesar, K. C. Balcomb, C. M. Gabriele, M. E. Dahlheim, S. Uchida, G. Ellis, Y. Mitamura, P. Ladron de Guevara, M. Yamaguchi, F. Sato, S. A. Mizroch, L. Schlender, K. Rasmussen, J. Barlow, and T. J. Quinn II. 2001. Movements and population structure of humpback whales in the North Pacific. *Marine Mammal Science* 17:769–794.

Calambokidis, J., G. H. Steiger, J. M. Straley, T. J. Quinn II, L. M. Herman, S. Cerchio, D. R. Salden, M. Yamaguchi, F. Sato, J. Urban, J. Jacobsen, O. von Ziegesar, K. C. Balcomb, C. M. Gabriele, M. E. Dahlheim, N. Higashi, S. Uchida, J. K. B. Ford, Y. Miyamura, P. Ladron de Guevara, S. A. Mizroch, L. Schlender, and K. Rasmussen. 1997. *Abundance and population structure of humpback whales in the North Pacific basin*. Contract No. 50ABNF500113, Southwest Fisheries Science Center, La Jolla, CA .

Cartwright, R. 1999. Factors affecting the behavior of humpback whale, *Megaptera novaeangliae*, calves whilst in Hawaiian waters. MS thesis, Manchester Metropolitan Univ., UK.

———. 2005. A comparative study of the behaviour and dynamics of humpback whale (*Megaptera novaeangliae*) mother and calf pairs during their residence in nursery waters. PhD diss., Manchester Metropolitan Univ., UK.

Cerchio, S. 1998. Estimates of humpback whale abundance off Kauai, 1989–1993: Evaluating biases associated with sampling the Hawaiian Islands breeding assemblage. *Marine Ecology Progress Series* 175:23–34.

Cerchio, S., C. Gabriele, T. F. Norris, and L. M. Herman. 1998. Movements of humpback whales between Kauai and Hawaii: Implication for the population structure and abundance estimation in the Hawaiian Islands. *Marine Ecology Progress Series*, 175:13–22.

Cerchio, S., J. K. Jacobsen, D. M. Cholewiak, E. A. Falcone, and D. A. Merriwether. 2005. Paternity in humpback whales, *Megaptera novaeangliae*: Assessing polygyny and skew in male reproductive success. *Animal Behavior* 70:267–277.

Cerchio, S., J. K. Jacobsen, and T. F. Norris. 2001. Temporal and geographic variation in songs of humpback whales (*Megaptera novaeangliae*): Synchronous change in Hawaiian and Mexican breeding assemblages. *Animal Behavior* 62:313–329.

Chadwick, D. H. 2007. What are they doing down there? *National Geographic* Magazine Jan. 2007:72–93.

Chittleborough, R. G. 1953. Aerial observations on the humpback whale *M. nodosa*. *Australian Journal of Marine and Freshwater Research* 9:1–18.

———. 1958. The breeding cycle of the female humpback whale *Megaptera nodosa* (Bonaterre). *Australian Journal of Marine and Freshwater Research* 9:1–18.

———. 1965. Dynamics of two populations of the humpback whale *Megaptera novaeangliae* (Borowski). *Australian Journal of Marine and Freshwater Research* 16:33–128.

Chu, K. C. 1988. Dive times and ventilation patterns of singing humpback whales (*Megaptera novaeangliae*). *Canadian Journal of Zoology* 66:1322–1327.

Chu, K. C., and P. Harcourt. 1986. Behavioral correlations with aberrant patterns in humpback whale songs. *Behavioral Ecology and Sociobiology* 19:309–312.

Clapham. P. J. 1992. Age of attainment of sexual maturity in humpback whales, *Megaptera novaeangliae*. *Canadian Journal of Zoology* 70:1470–1472.

———. 1993. The social and reproductive biology of North Atlantic humpback whales, *Megaptera novaeangliae*. PhD diss., Univ. of Aberdeen, Scotland.

———. 1996. The social and reproductive biology of humpback whales: An ecological perspective. *Mammal Review* 26:27–49.

———. 2002. Humpback whales. In *Encyclopedia of marine mammals*, eds. W. F. Perrin, B. Wursig, and J. G. M. Thewissen, 589–592. New York: Academic Press.

Clapham, P. J., and D. K. Mattila. 1990. Humpback whale songs as indications of migration routes. *Marine Mammal Science* 6:155–160.

Clapham, P. J., and C. A. Mayo. 1987. Reproduction and recruitment of individually identified humpback whales, *Megaptera novaeangliae*, observed in Massachusetts Bay, 1979–1985. *Canadian Journal of Zoology* 65:2853–2863.

———. 1990. Reproduction of humpback whales, *Megaptera novaeangliae*, observed in the Gulf of Maine. Special Issue, *Reports of the International Whaling Commission*, 12:171–175.

Clapham, P. J., P. J. Palsboll, D. K. Mattila, and V. Oswaldo. 1992. Composition of humpback whale competitive groups in the West Indies. *Behavior* 122:182–194.

Clapham, P. J., S. B. Young, and R. L. Brownell, Jr. 1999. Baleen whales: Conservation issues and the status of the most endangered populations. *Mammal Review* 29:35–60.

Clark, C. W., and P. J. Clapham. 2004. Acoustic monitoring of a humpback whale (*Megaptera novaeangliae*) feeding ground shows continual singing into late spring. *Proceedings Royal Society of London* 271:1051–1057.

Clutton-Brock, T. H. 1989. Mammalian mating systems. *Proceedings Royal Society of London* B 236:339–372.

Committee on Abrupt Climate Change and National Research Council. 2002. Abrupt climate change: Inevitable surprises. Washington, DC: *National Academy Press.*

Craig, A. S., and L. M. Herman. 1997. Sex differences in site fidelity and migration of humpback whales (*Megaptera novaeangliae*) to the Hawaiian Islands. *Canadian Journal of Zoology* 75:1923–1933.

———. 2000. Habitat preferences of female humpback whales, *Megaptera novaeangliae*, in the Hawaiian Islands are associated with reproductive status. *Marine Ecology Progress Series* 193:209–216.

Craig, A. S., L. M. Herman, C. M. Gabriele, and A. A. Pack. 2003. Migratory timing of humpback whales (*Megaptera novaeangliae*) in central North Pacific varies with age, sex and reproductive status. *Behavior* 140:981–1001.

Craig, A. S., L. M. Herman, and A. A. Pack. 2002. Male mate choice and male-male competition coexist in the humpback whale (*Megaptera novaeangliae*). *Canadian Journal of Zoology* 80:745–755.

———. 1983. Migrations, abundance and behavior of Hawaiian humpback whales (*Megaptera novaeangliae*). PhD diss., Univ. of California, Santa Cruz, CA.

———. 1984. Gray whales off Vancouver Island, British Columbia. In *The gray whale*, eds. M. L. Jones, S. Leatherwood, and S. Swartz, 267–287. New York: Academic Press.

Darling, J. D. 1990. *With the whales*. Minocqua, WI: Northword Press.

Darling, J. D., and M. Bérubé. 2001. Interactions of singing humpback whales with other males. *Marine Mammal Science* 17:570–584.

Darling, J. D., and S. Cerchio. 1993. Movement of a humpback whale between Japan and Hawaii. *Marine Mammal Science* 9:84–89.

Darling, J. D., and C. M. Jurasz. 1983. Migratory destinations of North Pacific humpback whales (*Megaptera novaeangliae*). In *Communication and behavior of whales*. AAAS Selected Symposia Series. ed. R. Payne, 359–368. Boulder, CO: Westview Press.

Darling, J. D., K. M. Gibson, and G. Silber. 1983. Observations on the abundance and behavior of humpback whales (*Megaptera novaeangliae*) off West Maui, Hawaii 1977–79. In *Communication and behavior of whales*. AAAS Selected Symposia Series. ed. R. Payne, 201–222. Boulder, CO: Westview Press.

Darling, J. D., M. E. Jones, and C. P. Nicklin. 2006. Humpback whale songs: Do they organize males during the breeding season? *Behavior* 143:1051–1101.

Darling, J. D., and D. J. McSweeney. 1985. Observations on the migrations of North Pacific humpback whales (*Megaptera novaeangliae*). *Canadian Journal of Zoology* 63:308–314.

Darling, J. D., and H. Morowitz. 1986. Census of "Hawaiian" humpback whales (*Megaptera novaeangliae*) by individual identification. *Canadian Journal of Zoology* 64:105–111.

Dawbin, W. H. 1966. The seasonal migratory cycle of humpback whales. In *Whales, dolphins and porpoises*. ed. K. S. Norris, 145–170. Berkeley: Univ. of California Press.

De Guise, S., D. Martineau, P. Beland, and P. Fournier. 1995. Possible mechanisms of action of environmental contaminants on St. Lawrence beluga whales (*Delphinapterus leucas*). *Environmental Health Perspectives* 103:73–77.

Dietz, T. 1982. *Tales of whales.* Portland, ME: Gannett Publishing Co.

Doroshenko, N. V. 2000. Soviet catches of humpback whales (*Megaptera novaeagliae*) in the North Pacific. In *Soviet whaling data* (1949–1979), 48–93. Moscow: Center for Russian Environmental Policy, Marine Mammal Council.

Elliott, W., and M. Simmonds. 2007. Whales in hot water? The impact of a changing climate on whales, dolphins and porpoises: A call for action. Chippenham, UK: WWF-International, Gland, Switzerland / WDCS.

Ellis, R. 1991. *Men and whales.* New York: Alfred A. Knopf.

Emlen, S. T., and L. W. Oring. 1977. Ecology, sexual selection, and the evolution of mating systems. *Science* 197:215–223.

Frankel, A. S., C. W. Clark, L. M. Herman, and C. Gabriele. 1995. Spatial distribution, habitat utilization, and social interactions of humpback whales, *Megaptera novaeangliae*, of Hawaii determined using acoustic and visual techniques. *Canadian Journal of Zoology* 73:1134–1146.

Frazer, L. N., and E. Mercado. 2000. A sonar model for the humpback whale song. *Journal of Oceanic Engineering* 25:160–181.

Gabriele, C. M. 1992. The behavior and residence characteristics of reproductive classes of humpback whales (*Megaptera novaeangliae*) in the Hawaiian Islands. MA thesis. Univ. of Hawaii, Honolulu, HI.

Gabriele, C. M., J. M. Straley, L. M. Herman, and R. J. Coleman. 1996. Fastest documented migration of a North Pacific humpback whale. *Marine Mammal Science* 12:457–464.

Gabriele, C. M., J. M. Straley, and J. L. Neilson. 2007. Age at first calving of female humpback whales in southeastern Alaska. *Marine Mammal Science* 23:226–239.

Glockner, D. A. 1983. Determining the sex of humpback whales (*Megaptera novaeangliae*) in their natural environment. In *Communication and behavior of whales*, ed. R. Payne, 447–464. AAAS Selected Symposia Series. Boulder, CO: Westview Press.

Glockner, D. A., and S. Venus. 1983. Identification, growth rate, and behavior of humpback whale (*Megaptera novaeangliae*) cows and calves in the waters off Maui, Hawaii 1977–79. In *Communication and behavior of whales*, ed. R. Payne, 223–258. AAAS Selected Symposia Series. Boulder, CO: Westview Press.

Glockner-Ferrari, D. A., and M. J. Ferrari. 1984. Reproduction in humpback whales, *Megaptera novaeangliae*, in Hawaiian waters. Special Issue, *Reports of the International Whaling Commission* 6:237–242.

———. 1985. Individual identification, behavior, reproduction and distribution of humpback whales, *Megaptera novaeangliae*, in Hawaii. Final Report U.S. Marine Mammal Commission, Contract MM2629752-5. Washington, DC: U.S. Marine Mammal Commission.

———. 1990. Reproduction in the humpback whale (*Megaptera novaeangliae*) in Hawaiian waters, 1975–1988: The life history, reproductive rates, and behavior of known individuals identified through surface and underwater photography. Special Issue, *Reports of the International Whaling Commission* 12:161–167.

Helweg, D. A. 1989. The daily and seasonal patterns of behavior and abundance of humpback whales (*Megaptera novaeangliae*) in Hawaiian waters. MA thesis, Univ. of Hawaii, Honolulu, HI.

Helweg, D. A., A. S. Frankel, F. R. Mobley, and L. M. Herman. 1992. Humpback whale song: Our current understanding. In *Marine Mammal Sensory Systems*, eds. J. Thomas et al., 459–483. New York: Plenum Press.

Helweg, D. A., and L. M. Herman. 1994. Diurnal patterns of behavior and group membership of humpback whales (*Megaptera novaeangliae*) wintering in Hawaiian waters. *Ethology* 98:298–311.

Herman, L. M. 1979. Humpback whales in Hawaiian waters: A study in historical ecology. *Pacific Search* 33:1–15.

Herman, L. M., and R. C. Antinoja. 1977. Humpback whales in the Hawaiian breeding waters: Population and pod characteristics. *Scientific Reports Whales Research Institute Tokyo* 29:59–85.

Herman, L. M., and W. N. Tavolga. 1980. The communications systems of cetaceans. In *Cetacean behavior, mechanisms and functions*, ed. L. M. Herman, 149–209. New York: John Wiley and Sons.

Hoyt, E. 2001. Whale watching 2001: Worldwide tourism numbers, expenditures, and expanding socioeconomic benefits. Yarmouth Port, MA: International Fund for Animal Welfare.

Jaquet, N. 2006. A simple photogrammetric technique to measure sperm whales at sea. *Marine Mammal Science* 22:862–879.

Jones, M. L., and S. L. Swartz. 1984. Demography and phenology of gray whales and evaluation of whale-watching activities in Laguna San Ignacio, Baja California sur, Mexico. In *The gray whale*, eds. M. L. Jones, S. J. Leatherwood, and S. L. Swartz, 289–307. New York: Academic Press.

Katona, S., B. Baxter, O. Brazier, S. Kraus, J. Perkins, and H. Whitehead. 1979. Identification of humpback whales by fluke photographs. *In Behavior of marine animals — current perspectives in research, Vol. 3: Cetaceans*. eds. H. E. Winn and B. L. Olla, 33–44. Plenum Press, N.Y.

Kellogg, R. 1928. What is known of the migrations of some of the whalebone whales. *Annual Reports Smithsonian Institution* 1928:467–494.

Krebs, J. R., and Davies, N. B. 1996. *Introduction to behavioral ecology*. Oxford, UK: Blackwell Scientific.

Lindbergh, J. 1967. Underwater is the right place to meet a whale. *Life* magazine December 1967:50–51.

Lockyer, C. 1981. Growth and energy budgets of large baleen whales from the southern hemisphere. In *Mammals in the seas*, Vol 3. 379–487. Rome: Food and Agricultural Organization of the United Nations.

Lockyer, C. 1984. Review of baleen whale (Mysticeti) reproduction and implications for management. Special Issue, *Reports of the International Whaling Commission* 6:27–48.

Lyman, E., and D. Mattila. 2007. *Summary of 2007 disentanglement season. Hawaiian Islands disentanglement network report*. Kihei, HI: Hawaiian Islands Humpback Whale National Marine Sanctuary.

Lyman, E., and D. Mattila. 2008. *Summary of 2007/2008 large whale entanglement and ship strike reports. Hawaiian Islands disentanglement network report*. Kihei, HI: Hawaiian Islands Humpback Whale National Marine Sanctuary.

Mate, B. R., R. Gisiner, and J. Mobley. 1998. Local and migratory movements of the Hawaiian humpback whales tracked by satellite telemetry. *Canadian Journal of Zoology* 76:863–868.

Mate, B. R., R. Mesecar, and B. Lagerquist. 2007. The evolution of satellite-monitored radio tags for large whales: One laboratory's experience. *Deep-Sea Research* II 54:224–247.

Matthews, L. H. 1937. The humpback whale, *Megaptera nodosa. Discovery Reports* 17:7–92.

Mattila, D. K., P. J. Clapham, S. K. Katona, and G. S. Stone. 1989. Population composition of humpback whales, *Megaptera novaeangliae*, on Silver Bank 1984. *Canadian Journal of Zoology* 67:281–285.

Mattila, D. K., L. N. Guinee, and C. A. Mayo. 1987. Humpback whale songs on a North Atlantic feeding ground. *Journal of Mammalogy* 68:880–883.

McSweeney, D. J., R. W. Baird, and S. D. Mahaffy. 2007. Site fidelity, associations and movements of Curvier's (*Ziphius cavirostris*) and Blainville's (*Mesoplodon densirostris*) beaked whales off the Island of Hawaii. *Marine Mammal Science* 23:666–687.

McSweeney, D. J., K. C. Chu, W. F. Dolphin, and L. N. Guinee. 1989. North Pacific humpback whale songs: A comparison of southeast Alaskan feeding ground songs and Hawaiian wintering ground songs. *Marine Mammal Science* 5:16–138.

Mead, J. G., and J. D. Gold. 2002. *Whales and dolphins in question. The Smithsonian answer book*. Washington, DC: Smithsonian Institution Press.

Medrano, L., M. Salinas, I. Salas, P. Ladron de Guevara, A. Aguayo, J. Jacobsen, and C. S. Baker. 1994. Sex identification of humpback whales, *Megaptera novaeangliae*, on the wintering grounds of the Mexican Pacific Ocean. *Canadian Journal of Zoology* 72:1771–1774.

Mesnick, S. 1997. Sexual alliances: Evidence and evolutionary implications. In *Feminism and evolutionary biology: Boundaries, intersections and frontiers*, ed. P. A. Gowaty, 207–257. New York: Chapman & Hall.

Mikhalev, Y. A. 2000. Biological characteristics of humpbacks taken in the Antarctic Area V by the whaling fleets Slava and Sovietskaya Ukraina. Paper IA12 submitted to the Scientific Committee of the International Whaling Commission (Unpublished, cited in Noad and Cato 2007).

Miller, P. J. O., N. Biassoni, A. Samuels, and P. L. Tyack. 2000. Whale songs lengthen in response to sonar. *Nature* 405:203.

Mobley, J. R., and L. M. Herman. 1985. Transience of social affiliations among humpback whales (*Megaptera novaeangliae*) on Hawaiian wintering grounds. *Canadian Journal of Zoology* 63:762–772.

Mobley, J. R., G. B. Bauer, and L. M. Herman. 1999. Changes over a ten-year interval in the distribution and relative abundance of humpback whales (*Megaptera novaeangliae*) wintering in Hawaiian waters. *Aquatic Mammals* 25:63–72.

Mobley, J. R., P. H. Forestall, and R. Grotefendt. 1994. Results of aerial surveys in Hawaiian waters. Annual report. Arlington, VA: Advanced Research Projects Agency.

Mobley, J. R., L. M. Herman, and A. S. Frankel. 1988. Responses of wintering humpback whales (*Megaptera novaeangliae*) to playbacks of winter and summer vocalizations and of synthetic sound. *Behavioral Ecology and Sociobiology* 23:211–223.

Nishiwaki, M. 1959. Humpback whales in Ryukyuan waters. *Scientific Reports of the Whales Research Institute Tokyo* 14:49–86.

———. 1960. Ryukyuan humpback whaling in 1960. *Scientific Reports of the Whales Research Institute Tokyo* 15:1–16.

————. 1962. Ryukyuan whaling in 1961. *Scientific Reports of the Whales Research Institute Tokyo* 16:19–28.

————. 1966. Distribution and migration of the larger cetaceans in the North Pacific as shown by Japanese whaling results. In *Whales, dolphins and porpoises*, ed. K. S. Norris, 171–191. Berkeley, CA: Univ. of California Press.

Noad, M. J., and D. H. Cato. 2007. Swimming speeds of singing and non-singing humpback whales during migration. *Marine Mammal Science* 23:481–495.

Noad, M. J., D. H. Cato, M. M. Bryden, M. N. Jenner, and C. S. Jenner. 2000. Cultural revolution in whale songs. *Nature* 408:537.

Pack, A. A., L. M. Herman, A. S. Craig, S. S. Spitz, and M. H. Deakos. 2002. Penis extrusions by humpback whales (*Megaptera novaeangliae*). *Aquatic Mammals* 28:131–146.

Pack, A. A., D. Salden, M. J Ferrari, D. A. Glockner-Ferrari, L. M. Herman, H. A. Stubbs, and J. M. Straley. 1998. Male humpback whale dies in competitive group. *Marine Mammal Science* 14:861–873.

Palsboll, P. 1999. Genetic tagging: Contemporary molecular ecology. *Biological Journal of the Linnean Society* 68:3–22.

Payne, R. S., and L. N. Guinee. 1983. Humpback whale songs as an indicator of "stocks." In *Communication and behavior of whales*. AAAS Selected Symposia Series, ed. R. Payne, 333–358. Boulder, CO: Westview Press.

Payne, R., and S. McVay. 1971. Songs of humpback whales. *Science* 173:585–597.

Payne, K. P., and R. S. Payne. 1985. Large scale changes over 19 years in songs of humpback whales off Bermuda. *Zeitschrift für Tierpsychologie* 68:89–114.

Payne, R., O. Brazier, E. M. Dorsey, J. S. Perkins, V. J. Rowntree, and A. Titus. 1983. External features in southern right whales (*Eubalaena australis*) and their use in identifying individuals. In *Communication and behavior of whales*. AAAS Selected Symposia Series, ed. R. Payne, 371–446. Boulder, CO: Westview Press.

Payne, K., P. Tyack, and R. Payne. 1983. Progressive changes in the songs of humpback whales (*Megaptera novaeangliae*): A detailed analysis of two seasons in Hawaii. In *Communication and behavior of whales. AAAS Selected Symposia Series*, ed. R. Payne, 9–57. Boulder, CO: Westview Press.

Perryman, W. L., and M. S. Lynn. 2002. Evaluation of nutritive condition and reproductive status of migrating gray whales (*Eschrichtius robustus*) based on analysis of photogrammetric data. *Journal of Cetacean Research Management* 4:155–164.

Rice, D. W. 1978. The humpback whale in the North Pacific: Distribution, exploitation and numbers. In Report on a workshop on problems related to humpback whales (*Megaptera novaeangliae*) in Hawaii, eds. K. S. Norris and R. R. Reeves, 29–44. Report MMC-77/03 to US Marine Mammal Commission, Washington D.C.

Rice, D. W., and A. A. Wolman. 1980. Census of humpback whales wintering around the Hawaiian Islands 1976–1979. Report to International Whaling Commission, Doc. No. Sc/31/38.

Ross, P. S., G. M. Ellis, M. G. Ikonomou, L. G. Barrett-Lennard, and R. F. Addison. 2000. High PCB concentrations in free-ranging Pacific killer whales, *Orcinus orca*: Effects of age, sex and dietary preference. *Marine Pollution Bulletin* 40: 504–515.

Rowntree, V., J. Darling, G. Silber, and M. Ferrari. 1980. Rare sighting of a right whale (*Eubalaena glacialis*) in Hawaii. *Canadian Journal of Zoology* 58:309–312.

Salden, D. R. 1990. Apparent feeding by a sub-adult humpback whale (*Megaptera novaeangliae*) off Maui, Hawaii. Report No. 4. Lahaina, HI: Hawaii Whale Research Foundation.

Salden, D. R. and J. Mickelson. 1999. Rare sighting of a North Pacific right whale (*Eubalaena glacialis*) in Hawaii. *Pacific Science* 53:341–345.

Salden, D. R., L. M. Herman, M. Yamaguchi, and F. Sato. 1999. Multiple visits of individual humpback whales (*Megaptera novaeangliae*) between the Hawaiian and Japanese winter grounds. *Canadian Journal of Zoology* 77:504–508.

Scammon, C. M. 1874. *The marine mammals of the northwestern coast of North America*. San Francisco, CA: John H. Carmany and Co.

Schofield, D. 2007. Pacific Islands Region marine mammal response network activity update, July 2007. Honolulu, HI: NOAA, Pacific Islands Regional Office.

———. 2008. Pacific Islands Region marine mammal response network activity update, January–April 2008. Honolulu, HI: NOAA, Pacific Islands Regional Office.

Silber, G. K. 1986. The relationship of social vocalizations to surface behavior and aggression in the Hawaiian humpback whale (*Megaptera novaeangliae*). *Canadian Journal of Zoology* 64:2075–2080.

Simao, S. M., and S. C. Moreira. 2005. Vocalizations of a female humpback whale in Arraial Do Cabo (R. J. Brazil). *Marine Mammal Science* 21:150–153.

Silvers, L. E., P. E. Rosel, and D. R. Salden. 2002. DNA sequence analysis of a North Pacific humpback whale (*Megaptera novaeangliae*) placenta. *Canadian Journal of Zoology* 80:1141–1144.

Silvers, L. E., and D. R. Salden. 1997. A large placenta encountered in the Hawaiian winter grounds of the humpback whale, *Megaptera novaeangliae*. *Marine Mammal Science* 13:711–716.

Smith, J. N., A. W. Goldizen, R. A. Dunlop, and M. J. Noad. 2008. Songs of male humpback whales, *Megaptera novaeangliae*, are involved in intersexual interactions. *Animal Behavior* 76:467–477.

Smultea, M. A. 1994. Segregation by humpback whale (*Megaptera novaeangliae*) cows with a calf in coastal habitat near the island of Hawaii. *Canadian Journal of Zoology* 72:805–811.

Spitz, S. S., L. M. Herman, and A. A. Pack. 2000. Measuring the sizes of humpback whales (*Megaptera novaeangliae*) through underwater videogrammetry. *Marine Mammal Science* 16:664–676.

Straley, J. M. 1999. Overwintering North Pacific humpback whales in Alaskan waters: Who are they? *Abstracts 13th Biennial Conference on the Biology of Marine Mammals*, Wailea, HI Nov. 28–Dec. 3, 1999.

Straley, J. M., C. M. Gabriele, C. S. Baker. 1994. Annual reproduction by individually identified humpback whales (*Megaptera novaeangliae*) in Alaskan waters. *Marine Mammal Science* 10:87–92.

Taber, S., and P. Thomas. 1984. Mother-infant interaction and behavioral development in southern right whales. *Behavior* 88:42–46.

Theodor, J. M. 2002. Artiodactyla. In *Encyclopedia of Marine Mammals*, ed. W. F. Perrin, B. Wursig, and J. G. M. Thewissen, 45–47. San Diego, CA: Academic Press.

Thompson, P. O., and W. A. Friedl. 1982. A long term study of low frequency sounds from several species of whales off Oahu, Hawaii. *Cetology* 45:1–19.

Tomilin, A. G. 1967. *Mammals of the U.S.S.R. and adjacent countries, Vol. 9. Cetacea* (trans. by O. Ronen from the 1957 Russian edition). Israel Program for Scientific Translations, Jerusalem.

Turvey, S. T., R. L. Pitman, B. L. Taylor, J. Barlow, T. Akamatsu, L. A. Barrett, X. Zhao, R. R. Reeves, B. S. Stewart, K. Wang, Z. Wei, X. Zhang, L. T. Pusser, M. Richlen, J. R. Brandon, and D. Wang. 2007. First human-caused extinction of a cetacean species. *Journal of the Royal Society, Biology Letters* 3:537–540.

Tyack, P. L. 1981. Interactions between singing Hawaiian humpback whales and conspecifics nearby. *Behavioral Ecology and Sociobiology* 8:105–116.

———. 1982. Humpback whales respond to sounds of their neighbors. PhD diss. Rockefeller Univ., New York.

———. 1983. Differential response of humpback whales, *Megaptera novaeangliae*, to playback of song or social sounds. *Behavioral Ecology and Sociobiology* 13:49–55.

Tyack, P., and H. Whitehead. 1983. Male competition in large groups of wintering humpback whales. *Behavior* 83:132–154.

Weller, D. W., B. Wursig, A. L. Bradford, A. M. Burdin, S. A. Blokhin, H. Minakuchi, and R. L. Brownell. 1999. Gray whales (*Eschrichtius robustus*) off Sakhalin Island, Russia: Seasonal and annual patterns of occurrence. *Marine Mammal Science* 15:1208–1227.

Wells, R. S., M. D. Scott, and A. B. Irvine. 1987. The social structure of free ranging bottlenose dolphins. In *Current Mammalogy Vol. 1*, ed. H. H. Genoways, 247–305. New York: Plenum Press.

Whitehead, H., and M. J. Moore. 1982. Distribution and movements of West Indian humpback whales in winter. *Canadian Journal of Zoology* 60:2203–2211.

Winn, H. E., and L. K. Winn. 1978. The song of the humpback whale, *Megaptera novaeangliae*, in the West Indies. *Marine Biology* 47:97–114.

Winn, H. E., W. L. Bischoff, and A. G. Turuski. 1973. Cytological sexing of cetacea. *Marine Biology* 23:343–346.

Winn, H. E., T. J. Thompson, W. C. Cummings, J. Hain, J. Hudnall, H. Hays, and W. W. Steiner. 1981. Song of the humpback whale — population comparisons. *Behavioral Ecology and Sociobiology* 8:41–46.

Wolman, A. A., and C. M. Jurasz. 1977. Humpback whales in Hawaii: Vessel census, 1976. *Marine Fisheries Review* 39:1–5.

Wrangham, R. W. 1986. Ecology and social relationships in two species of chimpanzees. In *Ecological aspects of social evolution in birds and mammals*, eds. D. I. Rubenstein and R. W. Wrangham, 354-378. Princeton, NJ: Princeton Univ. Press.

Wursig, B., and M. Wursig.1980. Behavior and ecology of the dusky dolphin, *Lagenorhynchus obscurus*, in the south Atlantic. *Fisheries Bulletin.* 77(4): 871–890.

Zoidis, A. M., M. A. Smultaea, A. S. Frankel, J. L. Hopkins, A. Day, A. S. McFarland, D. Fertl, and A. D. Whitt. 2008. Vocalizations produced by humpback whale (*Megaptera novaeangliae*) calves recorded in Hawaii. *Journal of the Acoustical Society of America* 123:1731–1746.

Website References

Convention on International Trade in Endangered Species of Wild Fauna and Flora (CITES). http://www.cites.org/

Government of Canada. Species at Risk Public Registry. http://www.sararegistry.gc.ca/approach/act/default_e.cfm

Greenpeace. http://www.greenpeace.org/international/

Hawaiian Islands Humpback Whale National Marine Sanctuary. http://hawaiihumpbackwhale.noaa.gov/

International Whaling Commission. http://www.iwcoffice.org/

Japan Whaling Association. http://www.whaling.jp/english/index.html

National Resource Defense Council. http://www.nrdc.org/

NOAA Fisheries Office of Protected Resource: Protection. http://www.nmfs.noaa.gov/pr/

NOAA Fisheries Office of Protected Resources: Hawaii Guidelines. http://www.nmfs.noaa.gov/pr/education/hawaii

Sheep101. Info: lambing. http://www.sheep101.info/lambing.html

Whale Trust. http://www.whaletrust.org

Sources

*See **References** for the full citations.*

Chapter 1 **Whales!**
What Are They Doing Out There? (e.g. Clutton-Brock 1989, Emlen and Oring 1977, Krebs and Davies 1996), **The 1970s** (e.g. Bigg et al. 1976, Darling 1984, Glockner and Venus 1983, Herman 1979, Katona et al. 1979, Payne et al. 1983, Rice 1978, Wells et al. 1987), *I Was the Intruder* (Lindbergh 1967), *List of Cetaceans in Hawaii* (Barlow 2006, McSweeney et al. 2007, Rowntree et al. 1980, Salden and Mickelson 1999), **How Have We Learned About Humpback Whales?**, **Whaling Studies** (Chittleborough 1958, 1965, Dawbin 1966, Matthews 1937, Nishiwaki 1959, 1960, 1962, 1966), **Studying Living Whales at Sea** (e.g. Barlow 2006, Darling et al. 2006, Mate et al. 2007, Palsbol 1999), *Whalers in Hawaii* (Ellis 1991, Herman 1979), **What Are Researchers Doing Out There?** (e.g. Amos 1997, Darling and Bérubé 2001, Glockner 1983, Jaquet 2006, Katona et al. 1979, Payne et al. 1983, Perryman and Lynn 2002, Silber 1986, Spitz et al. 2000), *Humpback Whales* (Calambokidis et al. 2008, Chittleborough 1958, Clapham 1996, 2002, Dawbin 1966, Nishiwaki 1959).

Social Groups on the Breeding Grounds (Baker and Herman 1984, Clapham et al. 1992, Darling 1983, Darling and Bérubé 2001, Darling et al. 1983, Gabriele 1992, Glockner 1983, Glockner-Ferrari and Ferrari 1985, Mobley and Herman 1985, Winn et al. 1973).

Chapter 2 **'Hawaiian' Humpbacks**
Hawaii — A Migratory Destination, Why Migrate?, North Pacific Humpback Whale Migrations, *Where Are the 'Hawaiian' Humpbacks in Summer?* (Baker et al. 1986, Calambokidis et al. 2001, Chadwick 2007, Chittleborough 1958, Darling and Cerchio 1993, Darling and Jurasz 1983, Darling and McSweeney 1985, Dawbin 1966, Gabriele et al. 1996, Kellogg 1928, Mate et al. 2007, Salden et al. 1999, Scammon 1874), **'Missing' Whales?** (Brown et al. 1995, Craig and Herman 1997, Lockyer 1981, Straley 1999), **Breeding And Nursery Grounds, Geography or Behavior?** (Brown and Corkeron 1995, Clapham and Mattila 1990, Clark and Clapham 2004, Craig and Herman 1997, Glockner and Venus 1983, McSweeney et al. 1989, Noad and Cato 2007), **Where are the Whales in Hawaii?** (Cerchio et al. 1998, Craig and Herman 1997, Frankel et al. 1995, Glockner and Venus 1983, Mate et al. 1998, Mobley et al. 1994, 1999, Rice and Wolman 1980, Wolman and Jurasz 1977), **When Is The Best Time to See Whales?** (Au et al. 2000, Baker and Herman 1981, 1984, Chittleborough 1958, 1965, Craig and Herman 1997, Craig et al. 2003, Darling 1983, Dawbin 1966, Gabriele 1992, Glockner-Ferrari and Ferrari 1985, Herman and Antinoja 1977, Jones M. pers. comm. 2001, Mobley and Herman 1985, Mobley et al. 1999, Nishiwaki 1959, 1966, Thompson and Friedl 1982), **How Long Does Any Individual Whale Stay In Hawaii?** (Darling 1983, Darling and Morowitz 1986, Gabriele 1992, Glockner and Venus 1983, Glockner-Ferrari and Ferrari 1985, Mate et al. 2007, Mobley and Herman 1985), **Whale Movements Within The Hawaiian Islands** (Baker and Herman 1981, Cerchio et al. 1998, Craig and Herman 1997, Darling and Morowitz 1986, Mate et al. 1998, 2007, Mobley et al. 1999), **Is There Location-Specific Activity In The Islands?** (Baker and Herman 1981, Craig and Herman 2000, Frankel et al. 1995, Glockner-Ferrari and Ferrari 1985, Mobley and Herman 1985, Smultea 1994).

Chapter 3 **Breeding Season**
Seasonal Cycles of Humpback Whales (e.g. Chittleborough 1958, Clapham 1996, Dawbin 1966, Lockyer 1984, Matthews 1937, Nishiwaki 1966), **How Have We Learned About Humpback Reproductive Cycles?** (Baker and Herman 1984, Baker et al. 1987, Chittleborough 1965, Clapham 1992, Clapham and Mayo 1987, 1990, Darling 1983, Dawbin 1966, Gabriele 1992, Glockner-Ferrari and Ferrari 1985, Matthews 1937, Nishiwaki 1959, 1960, 1962, 1966, Straley et al. 1994, Tomlin 1967, Tyack and Whitehead 1983), **Sexual Maturity And Birth Rate** (Baker et al. 1987, Barlow and Clapham 1996, Chittleborough 1958, 1965, Clapham and Mayo 1987, Clapham and Mayo 1990, Darling 1983, Gabriele 1992, Gabriele et al. 2007, Glockner and Venus 1983, Glockner-Ferrari and Ferrari 1984, 1985, 1990, Matthews 1937, Mobley and Herman 1985, Nishiwaki 1959, Straley et al. 1994), **When Mating Behavior and Pregnancies Don't Add Up** (Chittleborough 1958, Gabriele 1992, Glockner-Ferrari and Ferrari 1985, Mikhalev 2000 (in Noad and Cato 2007), Mobley and Herman 1985, Straley et al. 1994), **Mating Time, Estrus: Occurrence, Recurrence, and Duration** (Chittleborough 1958, 1965, Darling 1983, Dawbin 1966, Gabriele 1992, Glockner-Ferrari and Ferrari 1990, Matthews 1937, Mikhalev 2000 (in Noad and Cato 2007), Mobley and Herman 1985, Nishiwaki 1959, 1960, 1962, Tomlin 1967), **Estrus Cycles and Duration** (Sheep 101. Info (website), Theodor 2002), **Male Behavior Indicates Female Estrus** (Au et al. 2000, Baker and Herman 1984, Cartwright 1999, Darling 1983, Gabriele 1992, Glockner-Ferrari and Ferrari 1990, Mobley and Herman 1985), **How Do Male Whales Know a Female Is Ready to Mate?** (e.g. Krebs and Davies 1996, Mead and Gold 2002), **What We See And Why** (Baker and Herman 1984, Cartwright 1999, Craig et al. 2003, Darling 1983, Darling et al. 1983, Gabriele 1992, Glockner and Venus 1983, Glockner-Ferrari and Ferrari 1985, Mobley and Herman 1985, Tyack and Whitehead 1983).

Chapter 4 **Mating — The Male Perspective**
Singing, Escorting, Competing, And (Perhaps) Cooperating (Au et al. 2000, Baker and Herman 1984, Brown and Corkeron 1995, Clapham et al. 1992, Darling 1983, Darling et al. 1983, Darling and Bérubé 2001, Darling et al. 2006, Frankel et al. 1995, Gabriele 1992, Glockner-Ferrari and Ferrari 1985, Mobley and Herman 1985, Tyack 1981, 1983, Tyack and Whitehead 1983), **Male/Male Behavior, Singing** (Au et al. 2000, Clark and Clapham 2004, Darling 1983, Darling and Bérubé 2001, Darling et al. 1983, 2006, Glockner 1983, Glockner-Ferrari and Ferrari 1985, Mattila et al. 1987, McSweeney et al. 1989, Payne and McVay 1971, Payne et al. 1983, Smith et al. 2008, Winn and Winn 1978, Winn et al. 1973), **Bermuda and Whale Song** (Bermuda Zoological Society 1983, Dietz 1982), **The Song** (Cerchio et al. 2001, Noad et al. 2000, Payne and Guinee 1983, Payne and McVay 1971, Payne and Payne 1985, Payne et al. 1983, Winn et al. 1981), **Why Do They Sing?** (Au et al. 2000, Baker and Herman 1984, Brown and Corkeron 1995, Cerchio et al. 2001, Chu 1988, Chu and Harcourt 1986, Clapham 1996, Clapham and Mattila 1990, Clark and Clapham 2004, Darling 1983, Darling and Bérubé 2001, Darling et al. 2006, Frankel et al. 1995, Frazer and Mercado 2000, Helweg et al. 1992, Helweg and Herman 1994, Mobley and Herman 1985, Mobley et al. 1988, Noad et al. 2000, Payne et al. 1983, Silber 1986, Smith et al. 2008, Tyack 1981, 1983, Tyack and Whitehead 1983, Winn and Winn 1978), **Males Joining Singers** (Darling 1983, Darling and Bérubé 2001, Darling et al. 2006, Frankel et al. 1995, Helweg et al. 1992, Mobley et al. 1988, Smith et al. 2008, Tyack 1981, 1983), **Males Around Females, Accompanying a Female, What, Then, Is the Role of the Escort?** (Baker and Herman 1984, Chittleborough 1953, Clapham et al. 1992, Darling 1983, Darling et al. 1983, Frankel et al. 1995, Gabriele 1992, Glockner 1983, Glockner and Venus 1983, Glockner-Ferrari and Ferrari 1985, Herman and Antinoja 1977, Herman and Tavolga 1980, Mobley and Herman 1985, Tyack 1981, Tyack and Whitehead 1983), **Competition for Access to Females, Threats and Full-On Brawls** (Darling et al. 2006, Frankel et al. 1995, Glockner-Ferrari and Ferrari 1985, Mobley and Herman 1985, Mobley et al. 1988, Pack et al. 1998, Silber 1986, Tyack 1981, 1982, 1983, Tyack and Whitehead 1983), **Social Sounds** (Silber 1986, Tyack and Whitehead 1983), **Cooperation for Access to a Female** (Brown and Corkeron 1995, Clapham et al. 1992, Darling and Bérubé 2001, Darling et al. 2006, Frankel et al. 1995, Pack et al. 1998, Tyack and Whitehead 1983), Males Caring for

Other Males? (Pack et al. 1998).

Chapter 5 **Mating — The Female Perspective**
Pairing With, Avoiding and (Perhaps) Choosing Males (Baker 1985, Baker and Herman 1984, Clapham et al. 1992, Craig et al. 2002, Darling 1983, Emlen and Oring 1977, Gabriele 1992, Glockner 1983, Glockner-Ferrari and Ferrari 1985, Herman and Antinoja 1977, Mobley et al. 1988, Tyack 1981, Tyack and Whitehead 1983), **Female Roles** (Chittleborough 1965, Craig et al. 2002, Darling 1983, Dawbin 1966, Gabriele 1992, Glockner 1983, Glockner and Venus 1983, Glockner-Ferrari and Ferrari 1985, 1990), **What We See, Female with an Adult Male, Female with Multiple Males, Female Discouraging Males** (Baker and Herman 1984, Brown and Corkeron 1995, Clapham et al. 1992, Craig and Herman 1997, Craig et al. 2002, Darling 1983, Darling and Bérubé 2001, Darling et al. 1983, 2006, Gabriele 1992, Glockner-Ferrari and Ferrari 1985, Mattila et al. 1989, Mobley and Herman 1985, Mobley et al. 1988, Silber 1986, Tyack 1981, Tyack and Whitehead 1983), **What We Don't (or Rarely) See, Females Are Rarely Alone, Females Do Not Associate with Other Females, Females Do Not Join Singers,** *Copulation?* (Baker 1985, Baker and Herman 1984, Cartwright R. pers comm. 2001, Clapham et al. 1992, Darling 1983, Gabriele 1992, Glockner 1983, Glockner-Ferrari and Ferrari 1985, Herman and Antinoja 1977, Mobley et al. 1988, Pack et al. 2002, Smith et al. 2008, Tyack 1981, Tyack and Whitehead 1983), **Mating Situations,** *Rewinding History: When Does Mating Occur?* (Darling 1983), **Female/Male Pair, Females Leading Multiple Males** (Baker and Herman 1984, Chittleborough 1965, Clapham et al. 1992, Darling 1983, Darling and Bérubé 2001, Darling et al. 1983, 2006, Gabriele 1992, Glockner-Ferrari and Ferrari 1985, Mattila et al. 1989, Mobley and Herman 1985, Mobley et al. 1988, Silber 1986, Tyack 1981, Tyack and Whitehead 1983), **Do Females Choose Their Mates Based On Their Song?** (Chu 1988, Chu and Harcourt 1986, Clapham 1996, Clark and Clapham 2004, Darling and Bérubé 2001, Darling et al. 2006, Frankel et al. 1995, Gabriele C. pers. comm. 2001, Helweg et al. 1992, Mobley and Herman 1985, Medrano et al. 1994, Mobley et al. 1988, Smith et al. 2008, Tyack 1981, Tyack and Whitehead 1983, Winn and Winn 1978).

Chapter 6 **Newborns and Juveniles**
Maternal Priorities, Those Persistent Males, Avoiding the Neighbors, Predators (Chittleborough 1953, Darling 1990, Glockner and Venus 1983, Glockner-Ferrari and Ferrari 1985, 1990, Jones and Swartz 1984, Jones M. pers. comm. 2001, Nicklin F. pers. comm. 2000, Smultea 1994, Taber and Thomas 1984, Whitehead and Moore 1982, Wursig and Wursig 1980), **A Birth — Who Will See it First?** (Cartwright 2005, Chittleborough 1958, Darling 1983, Glockner-Ferrari and Ferrari 1985, Nishiwaki 1959, Silvers et al. 2002, Silvers and Salden 1997), **When Do We See Humpback Calves?** (Baker and Herman 1984, Craig and Herman 1997, Darling 1983, Gabriele 1992, Glockner 1983, Glockner and Venus 1983, Glockner-Ferrari and Ferrari 1985), **Newborns — How Do They Spend Their First Weeks In Hawaii?, Travel — The Most Common Activity!, Resting, Nursing, Play** (Cartwright 1999, 2005, Clapham 1996, Craig and Herman 1997, Darling 1983, Gabriele 1992, Glockner and Venus 1983, Glockner-Ferrari and Ferrari 1985, Mate et al. 1998, Mobley and Herman 1985), **Mother/Calf Communication** (Glockner-Ferrari and Ferrari 1985, Nicklin F. pers. comm. 2000, Simao and Moreira 2005, Zoidis et al. 2008), **The Calf And The Escort(s), Escorts: Are They Hired Guns?** (Cartwright 1999, Darling et al. 1983, 2006, Glockner-Ferrari and Ferrari 1985, Mesnick 1997, Mobley and Herman 1985, Wrangham 1986), **Juveniles** (Craig and Herman 1997, Darling 1983, Darling and Bérubé 2001, Dawbin 1966, Gabriele 1992, Glockner-Ferrari and Ferrari 1985, Salden 1989).

Chapter 7 **Whales and Us**
The 1900s, Whaling, Recovery, The Numbers (Baker and Herman 1987, Calambokidis et al. 1997, 2008, Cerchio 1998, Darling et al. 1983, Darling and Morowitz 1986, Doroshenko 2000, Herman and Antinoja 1977, Rice 1978, Rice and Wolman 1980), *Not All Whale Populations Are Recovering* (Best et al. 2001, Clapham et al. 1999, De Guise et al. 1995, Ross et al. 2000, Rowntree et al. 1980, Salden and Mickelson 1999, Turvey et al. 2007, Weller et al. 1999), **Hawaiian Humpbacks Today, The Promise — Science and Education, Protection, Science, Education, Whale Watching** (Convention on International Trade in Endangered Species of Wild Fauna and Flora (CITES) (website), Hoyt 2001, International Whaling Commission (website), NOAA Office of Protected Resources (website)), *The Hawaiian Islands Humpback Whale National Marine Sanctuary* (The Hawaiian Islands Humpback Whale National Marine Sanctuary (website)), *Approaching Whales in Hawaii* (NOAA Office of Protected Resources Marine Mammal Guidelines Hawaii (website)), **The Threats, Threats to Individuals: Entanglements and Collisions, Entanglements, Vessel–Whale Collisions** (Lyman and Matilla 2007, 2008, Schofield 2007, 2008), **Threats to Populations: Hunting, Food, and Habitat, Commercial Whaling, Competition with Human Fisheries, Changing Natural Habitats: Pollution to Climate Change, Cumulative Impacts — Adding Them All Together** (Clapham et al. 1999, Darling 1990, Greenpeace International (website), The International Whaling Commission (website), Japan Whaling Association (website)), *The Down-Listing and Whaling Debate* (San Jose Mercury News, June 8, 2007), *Extreme Noise Pollution: Naval Active Sonar Systems* (Miller et al. 2000, the National Resources Defense Council (website)), *Climate Change* (e.g. Committee on Abrupt Climate Change and National Research Council 2002, Elliott and Simmonds 2007).

Appendix **Agreements and Laws Protecting Humpback Whales**
(The International Whaling Commission (website), NOAA Office of Protected Resources (website), and the Government of Canada Species At Risk Public Registry (website)).

Actions and Postures
(Darling 1983, Gabriele 1992 (adapted from Bauer 1986 and Helweg 1989), Glockner-Ferrari and Ferrari 1985).

Index

*Numbers in **bold** are illustrations and tables.*

Biographies

Jim Darling

Jim began studying whales in the 1970s, developing individual photo-identification techniques for gray whales off Vancouver Island. His first experience with Hawaii's whales was during winter surfing trips, and this eventually led him to a PhD at the University of California Santa Cruz, researching humpback whale abundance and behavior. Since then, Jim has studied whales throughout the North Pacific and worldwide, but he returns to Maui annually to his focus on humpback singers and songs. Jim first met Flip Nicklin (an expert free diver) in Maui in 1979 and asked him to photograph singers without disturbing them.

Flip Nicklin

Flip's introduction to Maui's whales in the late 1970s inspired him to embark on a brilliant career in underwater photography. Since then, Flip has produced 20 *National Geographic* stories on whales and dolphins. He has set the bar not only for whale photography but also for photo-documentation assisting whale research. In winter, Flip can usually be found in his West Maui cottage, waiting for calm waters and, with Darling, still trying to understand what singers are doing out there. One wall of his cottage is adorned with three striking paintings that can be the work of only one artist — Sue Barnes.

FRAN GEALER

Susan Wallace Barnes

Sue grew up surfing in California and Hawaii in the late 1950s and early 60s, and she has never broken that tie with the ocean. Simply, Susan Wallace Barnes's art takes us to the beach and reminds us of its value. From her home above Carmel Bay (and one of the most beautiful beaches in the world), with whales often passing along its shores, she has spent a lifetime increasing public awareness and appreciation for the ocean. When asked to provide illustrations for this book, the answer was 'yes' in a millisecond, with the lament that she was not doing enough. . . .

ED LANE

WHALE TRUST

Making the world a better place.

RESEARCH • EDUCATION • CONSERVATION

www.whaletrust.org